BUDDHIST
INSPIRATIONS

BUDDHIST
INSPIRATIONS

TOM LOWENSTEIN

ESSENTIAL PHILOSOPHY,
TRUTH, AND ENLIGHTENMENT

DUNCAN BAIRD PUBLISHERS
LONDON

Buddhist Inspirations

First published in the United Kingdom and Ireland in 2005 by
Duncan Baird Publishers Ltd
Sixth Floor, Castle House
75–76 Wells Street
London W1T 3QH

Conceived, created and designed by
Duncan Baird Publishers

Senior Editor: Kirsten Chapman
Managing Designer: Dan Sturges
Picture Researcher: Susannah Stone
Commissioned artworks: Sally Taylor

Library of Congress Cataloging-in-Publication Data is available

Distributed in the United States by Publishers Group West

ISBN-10: 1-84483-116-7   ISBN-13: 9-781844-831166

10 9 8 7 6 5 4 3 2 1

Typeset in Myriad
Color reproduction by Scanhouse, Malaysia
Printed in Thailand by Imago

NOTES
The abbreviations CE and BCE are used throughout this book:
CE Common Era (the equivalent of AD)
BCE Before the Common Era (the equivalent of BC)

One of the gods came down to ask the Buddha:
"There's an inner tangle and an outer tangle.
This generation is entangled in a tangle.
Who will untangle this tangle of tangles?"
"Those established in morality and meditation,"
replied the Master, "untangle the tangle."

Jata Sutta

Contents

Introduction

Buddhism originated in India more than 2,500 years ago. But while this makes it the oldest of the world's major religions, the Buddhist Path remains as alive today as it was for its first followers. This can be explained by Buddhism's extraordinary adaptability and by its emphasis on inner experience. Thus the Buddha's teaching has spread to China, Japan, Tibet, Southeast Asia and now large parts of the West and, despite surface differences, has retained the same healing Word that is capable of transforming our lives.

Buddhism arose in an age that was restless, often sceptical, and in need of spiritual nourishment. Speaking at once to the head, heart and spirit, this may be why it retains its relevance and appeal today. Anyone, whether or not a declared Buddhist, can derive healing benefit from the Buddha's teaching – the proof of which lies in personal experience of it. The Buddha himself emphasized precisely this when he described his teaching as having the quality of *ehi-passaka*: "come-and-see-ness". Today this is just as possible as it was in ancient India – so read, contemplate and meditate.

The Buddha

"My teaching is about suffering and how to end it." So the Buddha, often described as the "great physician", once summarized his doctrine. Its overriding purpose was to diagnose and offer a remedy for the suffering of human experience. The Buddha, too, had suffered. His genius, however, lay in his ability to analyze and treat his own suffering, and then to show others how to follow his example and to achieve serenity and knowledge.

The Buddha did not start life as a religious adept. Originally a northern Indian prince by the name of Siddhartha Gautama, he became known as the Buddha (meaning "enlightened one") only when, as a relatively young man and through his own efforts, he became awakened to the nature of existence. What we know of his life before this has been recorded only in legends: these tell of his renunciation of a career at court, his marriage and the early years of his spiritual quest. Most of what we know about the Buddha dates from his adult years when he "shaved his head, put on a robe, took a begging bowl" and embarked on a life of poverty, meditation and teaching. Narratives of the Buddha's travels through the Ganges region are interwoven with the texts of his sermons. But what was new or different about the Buddha's message?

The Indian context

First, in addition to forsaking family and political life, the Buddha was reacting against the established religion of the period. Prince Siddhartha had grown up within the orthodox Brahmanic religion, whose rituals and worship of gods were of little interest to a mind focused on inner spiritual freedom. Nor did Hindu philosophers' emphasis on soul and divinity draw him.

But in reaction to the devotional and speculative sides of Hinduism, the young prince was not alone. The 6th century BCE was a period of great change and instability in northern India. Wars, natural disasters and famine had led to an unprecedented growth in urban populations and these factors, among many others, led to intellectual questioning and disquiet. Spiritual seekers were familiar figures at the time, many of them travelling the roads, practising harsh physical austerities, disputing with one another and proclaiming their discoveries. After leaving the palace Siddhartha adopted this wandering existence and strove, like many of his contemporaries, to uncover life's secrets, at first through punishing austerities and then through a less extreme "Middle Way".

The flood of *samsara*

What most of these ascetics also shared was a vision of life as just one stage in an interminable succession of rebirths into *samsara* – a condition often compared to a flooded and impassable river. How to reach the "other side" and the peace of *nirvana* (or "non-becoming") was the aim of both Hindus and independent thinkers like Siddhartha. The Buddha's genius was to arrive at a solution that depended not on adherence to an established religion, social status or caste but on subtlety of insight and personal effort. It is this that has inspired countless millions to embark on what later Buddhists called the "Ferry"or "Vehicle" of his teaching to cross the "ocean"of *samsara*. All of us live on this flood, and it is hoped that this book, which gives glimpses of the Buddha's career, his enlightenment and the central aspects of his teaching, will offer guidance and inspiration to those who wish to seek further.

After the death of the Buddha

The Buddha continued his life of teaching until the age of 80, and by the time of his death he had a large following of monks and lay people who helped to support the Sangha (monastic community). When the Buddha died this community needed to ensure that his teaching would be remembered and that the Sangha would remain intact.

Monuments containing the Buddha's cremated relics were erected as reminders of his doctrine. Soon after this 499 *arahats* (enlightened adepts) met to establish a canon of the Buddha's Dharma (teaching). Two senior monks recited from memory the monastic rules (*vinaya*) and the Master's sermons (*suttas*). Later a third group of teachings, the *Abhidharma*, was added to make up the three-part "basket" (*pitaka*) constituting the core of early Buddhist doctrine. For some 500 years these texts were memorized and transmitted orally until, in about the 1st century CE, they were finally written down in Pali, the literary language of Buddhism in Sri Lanka and Southeast Asia.

In the 3rd century BCE, a remarkable Indian Emperor, Ashoka, extended his rule from the kingdom of Magadha where the Buddha had taught, to the far north west and extreme south of India. Buddhism thrived and Ashoka attempted, often successfully, to rule with dharmic peace and justice. But Buddhism was not destined to survive in India. The deep-rooted Hinduism, which had preceded Buddhism, and Islamic conquests (8th–10th centuries CE) led to the extinction of Indian Buddhism by the 15th century.

The further spread of Buddhism

The texts written in Pali mainly represented the doctrine of the Theravada school of Buddhism, one of 18 sects that emerged in the 500 years after the Buddha's death. Theravada was probably the first school to carry Buddhism beyond the Indian mainland. Entering Sri Lanka in the 3rd century BCE, Theravada eventually became that country's majority religion and from there it was taken to Burma (Myanmar), Thailand, Laos and Cambodia – all these remain predominantly Theravadin.

Around the 1st century CE, new groups of Buddhists emerged who characterized their doctrines as the Mahayana, or "Great Vehicle". The term probably arose because Mahayanists considered Theravada and connected schools as being too restrictive as to the number of spiritual adepts who were admitted into the metaphorical ferry that crosses *samsara* and therefore referred to these other schools as Hinayana, meaning "Small Vehicle".

According to Mahayanists enlightenment is available to all beings, and new texts supporting this – many of which, it was claimed, had come from the Buddha himself – emerged from Mahayana monasteries. Another major aspect of Mahayana was the *bodhisattva* doctrine. In Mahayana terminology a *bodhisattva* is a being who is destined for enlightenment, but who has vowed not to enter *nirvana* until he has led all other beings to salvation.

The Mahayana had a profound effect on the sects that developed in China from about 50 CE, then in Korea and Japan in the 6th century CE, and finally in Tibet in the 7th century CE. This northerly spread of the Dharma brought about wonderful transformations in Buddhist thought, and many teachers from Tibet and Japan, such as the present Dalai Lama and, in the mid-20th century, D.T. Suzuki, have brought the Dharma close to us in the West.

The aim of this book is to inspire readers to seek further. Those with no previous knowledge of Buddhism may find ideas and activities in these pages which seem attractive and right for them. The Further Reading provides guidance on where to find out more. Buddhism is, above all, about exploring personal experience. The Buddhist Path is there for all to ponder or follow. All who wish may come and see! May all beings be happy!

CHAPTER ONE

LIFE AND INSIGHTS

Born into comfort and security, but

renouncing his inheritance, Siddhartha

Gautama was the prince who chose

poverty and wandering in the quest

for spiritual truth and tranquillity.

Early legends show us the extent

of Siddhartha's journey. Beautiful

accounts of his enlightenment reveal

the roots of human suffering and

open for us a path toward wisdom.

Samsara

In the time of the Buddha, most people in India believed that their lives in this world represented merely one stage in an infinite series of births. Any person's present life had been preceded by countless other lives; at death, the process would continue and the soul would migrate to yet another body. This might result in a new life as a human or as an animal.

This recurring pattern of events was known as *samsara*, a Sanskrit word meaning "eternal wandering". Far from delighting in the notion of repeated births, people feared it as a form of imprisonment – in some traditions *samsara* was represented by Yama, a terrifying Lord of Death (shown opposite).

Moving toward freedom

Before the Buddha many other thinkers had tried to solve the problem of how to escape *samsara*. Fortunately for us, the Buddha's solution has survived. Although more than 2,500 years old, it can still reach anyone today who is striving to understand their place in the world and in eternity.

The notion of *samsara* can be interpreted in many ways. As well as referring to past lives, it could describe the way we each go through our present life with problems that we have inherited or created in ourselves. As we progress we repeat the patterns that inhibit our happiness and spiritual growth. The teachings of Buddhism can help us to see our internal *samsara* and to clear a way through mental and emotional labyrinths of rebirth.

Karma

The Sanskrit word *karma* literally means "action" or "work". But in Buddhism the term suggests much more. The word *karma* describes the effect of our thoughts and intentional actions on our minds, hearts and bodies. Our personal *karma* is the result of these actions.

The Buddha explained that this *karma* keeps us in *samsara* – repeated rebirth into this world (see page 16). All beings, said the Buddha, are "heirs" or "children" of their *karma*. We are what we have made ourselves through our thoughts and actions, and the effects of what we have thought and done build up within us as we move through our present life. However, Buddhism also distinguishes between positive and negative *karma*. Wholesome actions, motivated by good will, generosity and spiritual awareness, generate good *karma* or merit. Actions that arise from greed, hatred and deluded thoughts create bad or unwholesome *karma*. Both positive and negative forms of *karma* affect the conditions of one's present life and the quality of one's rebirth.

Generating good *karma*

It is possible, however, to rid ourselves of bad *karmic* accumulations. Through mindful meditation (see page 75) and through positive actions – such as charitable works or giving alms – we can generate good *karma*, and this will in itself have a cumulative effect. With supreme generosity in one of his previous lives, the Buddha offered himself to a starving tiger and so reduced any remaining accumulations of *karma*.

Similarly, the more good *karma* we create, the less we will be inclined to generate bad *karma*. Ultimately, however, it is only if we shed all karmic accumulations that we would no longer experience rebirth into *samsara*, and so enter the deathless realm of *nirvana*.

Cause and effect

"All that we are is the result of what we have thought: it is founded on our thoughts, it is made up of our thoughts. If a person speaks or acts with an evil thought, pain follows him, as the wheel follows the foot of the ox that draws the wagon … If a person speaks or acts with a pure thought, happiness follows him, like a shadow that never leaves him."

The Buddha, the *Dhammapada*, c.5th century CE

The Prince Who Sought the Truth

The Buddha's personal name was Siddhartha Gautama, and he was born around the 6th century BCE into a family of rulers in what is now southern Nepal. According to legend his mother, Mahamaya, gave birth while standing, supporting herself with the branch of an overhanging tree. The infant Siddhartha emerged painlessly from her side. Within minutes he announced his intention to escape *samsara*. "I am born for enlightenment," cried the fully conscious child. "This is my last birth in the world of phenomena."

The questioning prince

Siddhartha's parents and the wise men of the court predicted a marvellous future for the child. He would become either a mighty world emperor or a great religious teacher. Anxious for the welfare of the kingdom, Siddhartha's father wanted his son to inherit the throne. But as the young prince grew, he showed no interest in court affairs. His inquiring mind sought just one thing: the answer to the question, "What is the meaning of worldly existence?"

Carving of the miraculous birth of Prince Siddhartha from Phnom Penh, Cambodia.

Fearing that Siddhartha might see too much of the world and that this would draw him into a quest to become a holy man, his father confined the young man to the royal palace. But, surrounded by beautiful women and pampered with soft living, Siddhartha grew restless. He knew that it was only by seeing and sharing life as it was lived by people outside that he could grapple with the nature of worldly existence.

The Four Sights

The term for the Buddha before his enlightenment is the Bodhisattva, meaning "enlightenment being". The Bodhisattva, like any other person, had to struggle hard for enlightenment. And before he could start that journey, he had to witness life outside the protective walls of his parents' palace.

The nature of the world

A beautiful but disturbing story recounts how the gods – who played only a small part in the Bodhisattva's world – arranged four dramatic scenes for the

A 19th-century Burmese manuscript illustration of Prince Siddhartha witnessing the Four Sights.

young prince to witness. These Four Sights imparted a tragic vision which it became the Bodhisattva's mission to transform and transcend.

The Four Sights were presented to Siddhartha as he was driven in a chariot through the palace park. The gods thought: "Soon the prince must attain enlightenment. We will show him a sign." So they made a god appear, ravaged by age, white-haired, toothless, broken down and trembling. The Bodhisattva asked his chariot driver, "What kind of man is that? He is unlike any I have seen." When his driver told him of old age, the prince cried: "Alas for birth, since all who are born must grow old!"

The path of renunciation

On his three next excursions, the gods showed the prince a sick man covered in sores, a corpse and the dead man's mourners, and lastly the figure of a homeless ascetic who wandered the world in tranquil poverty. Siddhartha asked his driver to explain this last vision. "This man, sir, has happily retired from the world." The thought of retirement pleased Siddhartha. This was the path he himself determined to follow.

In one of his sermons, the Buddha told his followers: "Thus while still a *bodhisattva*, I sought out the nature of birth, old age, sickness, death and sorrow, and having seen the misery that flows from these, I vowed to seek the supreme peace of *nirvana*."

The Great Departure

On the day that the Bodhisattva left the palace, he was presented with the vision of a holy man, which revealed that his wife had borne a son. He now faced a choice: either he must become a householder with a life subject to worldly restrictions or he must renounce conventional existence.

Turning away from sensuality

A Pali body of texts called the *Vinaya* describes how the Bodhisattva lay down to sleep. When he awoke his female attendants and musicians were asleep around him: "Some lay with their bodies wet with drool; some ground their teeth and muttered in their sleep; some lay with their mouths open; others lay with their clothes in disarray to reveal their nakedness." Finally convinced that a life of sensuality would lead to unhappiness, the Bodhisattva determined to leave and seek spiritual happiness in the "deathless state of *nirvana*".

Before he left, Siddhartha went to see his family. On a bed strewn with flowers, his wife and son slept, her hand on the baby's head. He knew that if he picked up his son, the queen would wake and prevent him from leaving. He left without waking them, vowing: "When I am a *buddha*, I will return."

Siddhartha left the palace with his groom Chandaka. At the city gate Siddhartha cut off his hair and beard and put on a yellow robe. Then he sent his groom back to the palace and began his homeless life alone. And so he found that "in the free air is freedom from the world".

A 10th-century Chinese painting of Prince Siddhartha and his groom, found in desert caves near Dun Huang, China.

The Bodhisattva's Search

Before he achieved enlightenment, the Bodhisattva led an extraordinary life. He left a palace for a life of homeless poverty. He studied with meditation masters; then, dissatisfied with their teaching, he joined a group of five ascetics who believed that mortifying the body would bring spiritual liberation.

Fruitless austerity

For six years the Bodhisattva meditated and starved, eating, so it is said, just one grain of rice a day. His body shrank and turned black. But this, thought the Bodhisattva, who was nearer death than spiritual illumination, was "like time spent endeavouring to tie the air into knots …"

Although these austerities had no ultimate value, they did teach him that extreme ascetism would bring him no closer to the truth than luxury. The discovery of a middle path took him to a new stage in his journey.

Approach to enlightenment

The Bodhisattva left his five companions. He went begging for food, and his body regained its shining golden colour. Shortly before the Bodhisattva's enlightenment, a young woman called Sujata learned that he had travelled to her area. She filled a bowl with rice milk and brought it to him. She paid him homage, saying: "Sir, accept this donation. May your wishes prosper like mine!" Strengthened with food, the Bodhisattva was ready for enlightenment.

Enlightenment Experience

After six years of wandering, the 34-year-old Bodhisattva had reached the kingdom of Magadha. As he came to the bank of a river, he thought: "Here is a delightful spot, with pleasant woods and water. This is a fit place to strive for enlightenment." Walking to a pipal tree, the Bodhisattva sat down. "I shall not move from this seat," he declared, "until I have attained absolute wisdom and the supreme state of peace." There he meditated for the next 49 days.

The Buddha's enlightenment took place in three watches. In the first he realized the impermanence of all things, in the second he surveyed five regions of rebirth, and finally he passed through eight stages of meditative trance. To celebrate his enlightenment, the gods suffused the earth with a rain of flowers and heavenly blessings. The Bodhisattva had become a *buddha*, an "Awakened One".

The insight to soothe all afflictions

"Just as a blind man might find a jewel amongst heaps of rubbish, so this spirit of awakening has somehow arisen in me. ... It is the supreme medicine that alleviates the illness of the world. It is the tree of rest for beings exhausted from wandering on the pathways of mundane existence."

Shantideva, the *Bodhicaryavatara*, 7th century CE

Mara, God of Darkness

Mara is the God of Death, the Evil One, the Tempter. He had followed the Bodhisattva from the moment he left the palace until the night of his enlightenment. Mara's aim was to divert the Bodhisattva from his spiritual destiny and so deprive the world of the Buddha who would teach salvation.

Assaults on the Bodhisattva

First, Mara promised the Bodhisattva a universal monarchy. When this failed, the god followed the Bodhisattva, trying at every opportunity to penetrate his will and concentration. The climax came in a spectacular assault as the Bodhisattva entered his enlightenment meditation.

The enraged Mara summoned his demons – grotesque armies of lust, aversion, craving, cowardice, doubt, hypocrisy, stupidity, false glory, and pride. Mara himself, with his thousand arms, rode a vast elephant. They unleashed winds, uprooted trees, hurled fire, sand and mud, and covered the earth with darkness. But the Bodhisattva sat unperturbed. Mara's daughters offered the Bodhisattva their bodies. But the Bodhisattva continued his meditation. "Yield your place to me!" screamed Mara in fury, "that seat is mine!"

The Bodhisattva's response was simply to stretch out his right hand and touch the earth. The earth roared, "I bear witness to the future Buddha!" Mara's army melted away. As the Evil One retreated, he wrote on the ground, "The holy Bodhisattva has escaped my kingdom!"

Past Lives

As part of his enlightenment, the Buddha saw his own past lives, and there are more than 500 *Jataka* (birth stories), describing his previous incarnations. In some he is an animal such as a tiger or monkey; in others he is a noble prince. Each story shows his increasing generosity and self-sacrifice, leading toward his final birth as the Buddha.

In one previous incarnation the Buddha had been Sumedha, a rich Brahmin. Sumedha lived at the time of another *buddha*, Dipankara (see below). One day Dipankara was approaching Sumedha's district, but the road was unfinished. Although he was high-caste, Sumedha lay on the ground rather than allow the *buddha* to tread on the hard earth. It was at this moment that Sumedha determined to become a *buddha* himself.

OTHER *BUDDHAS*

There were other *buddhas* who existed before the Buddha, and there will be other *buddhas* in the future. Some stories list the names of more than a hundred previous *buddhas*. One of these, called Dipankara, the Enlightener, was born in the mythological city of Depavati. He was given the name Dipankara because at the moment of his birth there was a miraculous manifestation of a multitude of bright *dipa* ("lamps").

The Noble Truths

There is nothing paranormal or other-worldly about the Buddha's realization as he sat under the pipal tree. His insights, on the contrary, were down-to-earth and realistic. But so radical were these insights that they transformed him, and with this awakening he liberated himself from suffering and rebirth.

The great physician

At the heart of the Buddha's enlightenment was his understanding of human experience, of what it feels like to be a person. The enlightened Buddha is sometimes described as the "great physician", and his first meditative realization does take the form of a diagnosis and cure. The Buddha identified the illness that afflicts humankind, and, by doing this, he was able to provide a remedy. This remedy, known as the Four Noble Truths, lies at the centre of Buddhist teaching.

The First Noble Truth

The Buddha's first insight was that all humans experience their lives as painful and unsatisfactory. He outlined this like a doctor identifying an illness:

What is the Noble Truth about Suffering (dukkha)? Birth is suffering, old age is suffering, death is suffering, grief, lamentation, discomfort, unhappiness and despair are suffering. To want something and not to obtain it is suffering …

The Second Noble Truth

With the Second Noble Truth the Buddha diagnosed the cause of suffering, the universal condition:

> *And what is the Noble Truth about the Origin of Suffering? It is craving that leads to rebirth, combined with pleasure and emotion, finding pleasure now here and now there, the craving for sensual experience, the craving for existence and also for non-existence ...*

The Third Noble Truth

But there is a way to free ourselves, declared the Buddha. In the Third Noble Truth he proclaimed:

> *What is the Noble Truth about the Cessation of Suffering?*
> *Indifference to desire and freedom from desire.*

With the Fourth Noble Truth (see following pages), the Buddha determined the cure: the Middle Way or the Eightfold Path, which help to lead to the cessation of suffering.

The Fourth Noble Truth

The first three Noble Truths (see previous pages) may initially sound negative or life-denying. But the Buddha's message in the Fourth Noble Truth reveals a life-enhancing wisdom. This truth provides guidance on how we can modify our thoughts and actions so as to achieve a life of happiness and freedom.

The Middle Way

As a Bodhisattva the Buddha had discovered that it was best to find spiritual insight by following the "Middle Way" between the luxury of his early palace experience and the asceticism of his six-year search. Having eaten sufficiently (see page 26) before he sat down to his enlightenment meditation, the Buddha went deeper into an exploration of the Middle Way. The result of this meditation was the Fourth Noble Truth: the Eightfold Path.

The Eightfold Path

The Buddha's teaching (the Dharma) is often represented by an eight-spoked wheel. Each spoke on this wheel represents an ideal. When combined, these ideals can offer a "cure" for the endless cycle of suffering, desire and rebirth.

The Buddha declared that in all our thoughts and actions we should strive to become balanced, harmonious, skilful or "just right". On the following page, the factors of the Buddha's Eightfold Path are outlined. Each is followed by a short explanation:

Right view or understanding. This brings us closer to the Buddha's teaching (the Dharma).

Right thought or intention. This requires that we bend our will and understanding to the Dharma.

Right speech. This encourages us to speak without falsehood and malice.

Right action. This suggests that we should be honest and non-violent.

Right livelihood. This asks us to pursue a life free from greed, hurtful behaviour, or exploitation.

Right effort. This means that we should use our energies in a balanced and skilful way.

Right awareness. This suggests that we should develop an alertness both to our inner processes and to outward events.

Right concentration. This reminds us that our meditation should always be focused.

The first two factors of the Eightfold Path tell us how we can develop wisdom; the third, fourth and fifth describe the things we should consider if we want to lead an ethical life. The last three factors detail the best ways in which to meditate.

The Buddha's Life in the World

The Buddha's adult life was spent walking through northern India, meditating in forests and even swimming across swollen rivers, so he must have been a robust figure. In this way he lived very much in the physical world. By contrast, renouncing his caste identity and choosing the life of a wanderer put him at the edges of the social world. But this was what he wanted. "Like a lotus," he said, "I was born in the world, but am unblemished by the world."

The travelling teacher

An 8th-century banner showing the Buddha preaching, found in caves near Dun Huang, China.

For the 60 years of his mission, the Buddha led a simple but organized life. This involved meditation, training his community and travelling to cities where he could teach. As the Buddha's message spread, his community attracted support. Donations of dwellings from merchants, landowners and even the King of Magadha, a kingdom in the Ganges valley, allowed the community to spend the rainy season in parks outside the towns, where the Buddha could lecture, answer questions and hold debates.

His mission to share

There were many rival teachers on the roads of India. But self-confident and sometimes sharp-tongued, the Buddha had a spiritual energy, which still shines through in his words. His compassionate mission was to bring enlightenment to those who had "only a little dust in their eyes".

Death of the Buddha

The young Siddhartha had embarked on his journey to solve the problem of suffering and death. Ordinary people, he had reasoned, were subject not only to death but to the pain of rebirth. Following his own enlightenment, the Buddha himself would never be reborn. For the rest of his 80 years, he therefore lived in a serene condition of "living *nirvana*". Part of his happiness lay in the confidence that he would not suffer rebirth.

Last days

In the Buddha's later life he continued to walk long distances, but he was sick and in need of rest. In conversation with his attendant Ananda, he said movingly: "I am 80. My body is like an old cart held together with straps. Only when I am in meditation is my body comfortable."

As the Buddha approached death, he repeated his whole doctrine to his followers. He warned them not to rely on his presence. "Be your own lamps," he said. "Be your own refuge." And in response to Ananda's bitter grieving, the Buddha reminded him, "The nature of things dictates that we must leave those dear to us."

A final meal

The Buddha's last meal was donated by a blacksmith, called Chunda, and the Buddha divined that one of the meat dishes was tainted. Out of respect for the offering and in the certainty that it would poison him, the Buddha ate his portion and ordered the rest of the meat to be buried. An agonizing sickness followed. But the Buddha's peace of mind was unshaken.

The Buddha's final words were: "Monks, do not grieve. Even if I lived an eon, my life with you would have to end. This in the nature of things. Practise with effort, destroy ignorance and seek your liberation. All conditioned things are subject to decay. Strive diligently!"

WISDOM'S ECHOES

The Awakened One, his teaching and the Buddhist community are the "Three Jewels" at the heart of Buddhism. Everything in the religion's tradition flows from the Buddha's insights. In this chapter you will hear echoes of the Buddha's own voice and the voices of those who perpetuated his wisdom. All are quietly eloquent, but they carry a great distance.

In the Deer Park

The Buddha spent seven weeks by the pipal tree – henceforth known as the *bodhi* tree (the tree of enlightenment, see page 113). The Buddha then faced a dilemma. Should he keep his profound new insights to himself or should he teach them to the world?

At first he was inclined not to proclaim his subtle new doctrine. He believed that his insights were unique. He had struggled over many lifetimes and through much self-training to understand them and he doubted that words could express what he had experienced.

The compulsion to teach

Legend tells us that when the deities got wind of his hesitation, the god
Brahma visited the Buddha and said: "Now, O sage, that you have yourself
crossed the Ocean of Becoming, please rescue the other beings who have
sunk low in suffering!" An inner impulse also persuaded the Buddha to teach:
he remembered that in his past lives he had promised to enlighten all beings.

The Buddha's first sermon

Still alone, the Buddha wandered to a deer park outside the small town of
Sarnath. Here he met the five half-starved ascetic companions with whom
he had studied before he had found the Middle Way. When they saw how
his body had been restored to health following its formerly shrunken state,
they mocked him for straying from the path of renunciation. But the Buddha
shone with such radiant light that they were soon convinced that he had
mastered the truth and attained *nirvana*.

   The Buddha then taught them his insights, describing the nature of reality
as summarized in the Four Noble Truths (see pages 34–7). So effective was
his teaching that all five listeners were enlightened and attained *nirvana*
themselves. These were the first members of the Buddha's monastic
community. The sermon at Sarnath is known as the First Turning of the Wheel
of Dharma – the Buddha's message had started to move into the world.

The Sangha

The three great pillars of Buddhism are: the Buddha, the Dharma and the Sangha. During the Buddha's lifetime, the Sangha consisted of his followers, who included monks, nuns and lay devotees. These lay people were householders, families, anyone who associated themselves with the Buddha's teaching or supported the monastic community with gifts.

Buddhist nuns chanting in unison. They are dressed in the white robes of the Thai Theravada tradition.

Of course, without the Buddha there would be no Dharma. But the Buddha regarded his followers as hugely important. In response to the question "Which of the three, Buddha, Dharma or Sangha, is the most important?" the Buddha replied: "the Sangha." Perhaps he meant by this that mutual support would help people to achieve enlightenment and to spread the Dharma.

JOINING THE BUDDHIST COMMUNITY

Not everyone has the opportunity of joining a Buddhist community or meditation centre. But there are growing numbers of Dharma groups throughout the world, and the evolution of the internet has made it increasingly possible to "visit" monasteries, temples and meditation groups – anyone can tap into the world-wide Sangha through the internet. Even if you follow the Dharma alone, meditation and devotion make you a part of the wider Buddhist community.

The *Fire Sermon*

Thought to have been delivered soon after the Buddha's enlightenment, the dramatic *Fire Sermon* is about the fires of passion that burn inside us all. Its highly poetic imagery still resonates today. The Buddha begins by saying that everything is on fire. But as the discourse continues, we can see that what he means is that we ourselves are on fire:

> *"All things are on fire. Forms are on fire. The eye, all the organs of sense, the body and the mind are on fire. Pleasant and unpleasant sense impressions are on fire. And what are these on fire with? They are on fire with passion, infatuation, aversion, hatred. They are on fire with birth, old age, death. They are on fire with sorrow, lamentation, misery, grief and despair."*

Extinguishing the flames

Far from condemning people because they are "ablaze" in this way, the Buddha is diagnosing a problem. Our internal flames make us suffer, but there is a way of extinguishing them. Through effort, mindfulness and understanding people can develop a clear view of their own personal fire. And when people perceive the nature of their flames, and then cultivate detachment and equanimity, the fire will die. The Buddha's teaching leads us toward a cool space within ourselves. It is no accident that the basic meaning of *nirvana* is "blowing out of fire".

Nirvana

Everyone has heard of *nirvana*. It is one of those Buddhist terms that has entered the modern vernacular. We might use it generally to refer to something wonderful that has happened or to describe an intense personal happiness, such as a perfect drink after long thirst, a holiday in the sun after a stressful winter, or the ecstasy of love or sexual fulfilment. But while it is good that this beautiful word should have entered modern thinking, using *nirvana* in these contexts almost exactly reverses its original meaning.

No wanting, no self

In Buddhism *nirvana* is a state in which any idea of the self has been obliterated. Instead of referring to personal satisfaction in the world, *nirvana* is the absence of desire for worldly gratification. Happiness comes not from getting something, but from no longer wanting anything. This extinction of wanting and of selfhood is in itself a living *nirvana*. At death this "non-self" cannot be reborn. This was exemplified in the Buddha: his life was his final incarnation, and while his life in the world was in itself *nirvana*, at death he entered a completed *nirvana*.

Another helpful way of thinking of *nirvana* is to contemplate the idea behind the Sanskrit word. Literally *nirvana* means "blowing out of fire". *Nirvana* is thus a cooling off. When we take the "heat" out of our passions, then a wonderful serenity can start to take over. This may be a taste of what the Buddha meant when he defined *nirvana*: "It is peace. The absolute. The end of the formations of the human personality. The end of every trace that could be reborn. The death of craving. Detachment. Extinction."

The absence of form

When the Buddha spoke of the "absolute", perhaps he referred to a condition that is here already, if only we could see and experience it. *Nirvana* exists in the absence of worldly forms that arise and die. *Nirvana* is: "Unborn. Unoriginated. Uncreated. Unformed. If the unborn, uncreated, unformed did not exist, escape from the world of the born, created and formed would not be possible." Hard as it is for us to understand these ideas, the Buddha would not have spoken of *nirvana* if it were not attainable. *Nirvana* is there. The Buddha's life and teaching show us the way.

The *Raft Sutra*

As the Buddha travelled in order to teach, he was often held up by rivers that were so dangerously swollen during the monsoon that no one could see to the far shore. Struggling across such swollen, turbulent waters, said the Buddha, was just like the voyage of life and rebirth in *samsara*.

Crossing the flood

This side of the flood – life as we know it – is dangerous and filled with suffering. The other side – distant and invisible – is *nirvana*. What are we to do? In one famous discourse the Buddha asked us to imagine that his teaching was like a raft that a man makes for crossing a terrible flood:

> *"Suppose this man comes to the flood. The near shore is dangerous and he wants to get to the other side where he will be safe. He thinks: 'If I collect branches and leaves to make a raft, after making a huge effort I could get to the far shore.' He does just this. But when he has arrived, he might think: 'The raft has been helpful. I shall I continue my journey with it.'*
> *Would that man be doing the right thing? Or should he set the raft adrift, and continue on foot?"*

The answer is obvious – the interpretation less so. Yes, the Dharma is like a raft. But, said the Buddha, "It is for crossing over with: not for grasping onto!"

Striving self-sufficiently

The story conveys two powerful messages. First, it is up to us as individuals to make our own use of the Dharma. Teachers can show us the "materials" from which to construct our rafts, but then we must do the hard work ourselves. No one, after all, can achieve enlightenment for us.

The second message is not to cling to the Dharma. It is a means of salvation, not an end in itself. Clinging to the Buddha's teaching involves the same process as clinging to the unwholesome things that make us suffer. The Buddha concluded: "When you understand the Dharma is like a raft, you should abandon all mental states, even good ones."

Three Characteristics of Existence

One of Sri Lanka's most senior monks, the Venerable Anandamaitreya Mahanayake, was once giving a talk on suffering, impermanence and *anatta* (absence of self). He described how these "Three Characteristics of Existence" are fundamental to Buddhism. But this seemed strange to some listeners, as the monks who spend their lives contemplating these negative concepts are generally such merry people. The speaker, then in his 90s, was no exception: humour and self-confidence flowed from every gesture; death held no terror.

Accepting the nature of life

How, asked someone, could such a life-loving man define life as suffering? "It is and it isn't," was his careful response. "When you see that everything is impermanent, then you also perceive that life as we conventionally experience it is unsatisfactory. And most people do suffer. That is the nature of our world and most lives. And since rebirth, mine and yours, is certain, we are a long way from *nirvana*! Only in *nirvana* is there no suffering at all."

To observe impermanence is only the first step toward accepting the transient nature of our lives. Every moment, however uneventful, is different. Our lives and surroundings are in perpetual flow. Comprehension of this helps to unlock the mystery of the third characteristic: *anatta*.

On one level, this explains the Buddha's disagreement with the Hindu and yogic emphasis on the soul and the self. He disliked mystical or supernatural speculation. On that level *anatta* means "no self, no soul". On a deeper level, however, *anatta* tells us that we are not exactly what we think. When we look into our identities we see that they have no centre. We are a mass of elements, events and histories.

"Which part of me," asked the Venerable Anandamaitreya Mahanayake, "is me? My memories, education, robe?" Then: "Is it my thumb?!" But, diving briefly into the realm of quantum physics, he concluded, "Isn't this thumb, like yours, just electrons and protons in whirling, transitory process?"

The Law of Causality

In addition to the Four Noble Truths, the Eightfold Path and the Three Characteristics of Existence, the Buddha's enlightenment experience contained a fourth major element. This was the Buddha's insight into the Law of Causality (*paticca-samuppada*), a realization that was connected to *karma* theory.

Karma is the process through which our actions accumulate residues in the psyche, which have an effect on how we are reborn in the next life (see pages 18–19). Through step-by-step analysis, the Buddha expanded on this concept and revealed exactly what it is that leads to *karma*-producing actions, as well as the repercussions that ensue. Some of the concepts in *paticca-samuppada*, such as the idea of "*karma* formations" (*sankhara*) and "sensory bases" (*ayatana*), may be puzzling at first. But once studied carefully, the Buddha's explanation of this chain of causality makes perfect psychological sense.

The chain of events

The Buddha's law is as follows:

    Through ignorance, rebirth-producing *karma* formations arise.

    Through *karma* formations, consciousness arises.

    Through consciousness, mental and physical phenomena arise.

    Through mental and physical phenomena, the sensory bases arise.

    Through the sensory bases, contact arises.

    Through contact, feeling arises.

    Through feeling, craving arises.

    Through craving, attachment arises.

    Through attachment, the process of becoming arises.

    Through the process of becoming, rebirth arises.

    Through rebirth, old age, death, pain, grief and despair arise.

Breaking the chain

Spiritual ignorance is at the start of the linked sequence and, as you can see above, this eventually leads to cravings and attachment and then on to suffering and rebirth. However, once we understand the Buddha's Dharma thoroughly, we may arrive at wisdom. Wisdom effectively reverses the causality process and there is no more rebirth.

Seven Factors of Enlightenment

Before he died the Buddha summarized for the last time the essence of his teaching and this included what he called the Seven Factors (or Branches) of Enlightenment. Like the Eightfold Path, these were ideals that people could strive to achieve. The factors he named were: awareness, exploration of the Dharma, energy, joy, serenity, concentration and equanimity.

Perhaps the most unexpected aspect of this grouping is joy. But joy is an experience that the seasoned practitioner feels during meditation, and is also a product of having lived according to the Buddha's Dharma.

Healing powers

At the time of the Buddha, the Seven Factors were associated with healing. On one occasion a monk, called Kassapa, was taken ill while meditating in a cave. The Buddha visited him and asked after his health. "I am in great pain," answered Kassapa. "It is no better." The Buddha then expounded the Seven Factors of Enlightenment and Kassapa was immediately cured of his illness.

A 6th–7th century Burmese stone carving showing the Buddha in the position of calling the earth to witness (see page 110).

On a later occasion, when the Buddha himself fell ill, one of his followers, perhaps remembering Kassapa's recovery, recited the same teaching, and the Buddha, too, was cured.

The Buddha once described this powerful effect: "Just as the rafters of a roof all slope toward the peak, so anyone who cultivates the Seven Factors of Enlightenment slopes toward and tends toward *nirvana*."

The Six Perfections

A life of virtue and meditation build on one another, and teachers in the Hinayana Buddhist tradition (see page 12) tell us that these two paths lead to wisdom. Later teachers of the Mahayana school (see page 12) expanded this formula into the "Path of the Six Perfections". These Perfections, also called "Attainments", are given as: generosity, morality, patience, energy, meditation and wisdom.

Generosity means giving, both in terms of material donations and one's own time, energy and love. The moral life implies sexual continence, non-violence, honesty, and decency of speech. Patience involves the development of equanimity in the face of suffering and enjoyment. Energy is about putting effort into spiritual endeavour. These, in combination with meditation, lead to wisdom and, eventually, enlightenment and buddhahood. But the Six Perfections are also dependent on each other: one or two without the others make a shaky edifice.

The Bodhisattva Path

Another description of the Path of the Six Perfections is the "Bodhisattva Path". In the

Mahayana tradition a *bodhisattva* is a saintly being who gives up the prospect of his own *nirvana* in order to bring enlightenment to others. This generosity is the ultimate characteristic of a *bodhisattva*. This is one reason why generosity lies at the head of the list of the Six Perfections.

BECOMING GENEROUS

There are many easy ways to become more generous in your everyday life. Here are a few suggestions:

1 It is helpful to imagine life from another person's point of view. When you next have a conversation, think how your words and actions affect the other person. Be considerate. Listen to them and value what they say. Extend this to all your conversations.

2 When our energy is in short supply we tend to economize on how much time we spend with our friends and family. Make extra space in your life for giving your love and friendship to the maximum.

3 Most people are short of money. But there are almost always people and communities in much greater need than you. Contribute to a reputable charity and take an interest in the work it does.

Perfection of Wisdom

Philosophy sometimes goes hand in hand with colourful mythology. For example, the *Perfection of Wisdom Sutras* were said to have been the words of the Buddha which were rediscovered 800 years after his death. It is said that he believed these teachings were too advanced, so they were carried to the kingdom of the serpents, until the sage Nagarjuna could retrieve them.

The double nature of things

These texts, which include the *Diamond Sutra* and the *Heart Sutra*, contain much profound teaching. One theme is that all things are essentially devoid of character: they are "empty". But, while everything is an "unreal dream", real compassion must still be extended to all beings. The *Diamond Sutra* contains the *bodhisattva*'s vow: "I vow to lead all beings to *nirvana*. Yet, even if innumerable beings are led to *nirvana*, no being has been led to *nirvana*."

There is another lovely contradiction. These difficult texts analyzing the mysterious, paradoxical nature of reality were also used as protective chants.

A spell of great knowledge

Ga-te! Ga-te! Paraga-te! Parasamga-te! Bodhi svaha!

Gone! Gone! Gone utterly beyond! Homage to wisdom!

The *Heart Sutra*, c. 1st century BCE

Emptiness

The Buddha once observed one of his disciples, Sariputra, as he emerged from meditation and remarked that his face shone with happiness and serenity. "What condition are you in, Sariputra?" enquired the Master. "Sir," replied Sariputra, "I am in a condition of emptiness." "Well done, Sariputra," responded the Buddha, "emptiness is the best of all states."

The English word "emptiness" often suggests an absence of meaning and is therefore a somewhat misleading translation for the Buddhist term *sunyata*. Buddhist emptiness, far from suggesting meaninglessness, points to the ultimate freedom contained in the realm of absolute truth. This truth is birthless and deathless. Like space, it has no character.

Understanding "no-self"

In worldly reality all things appear to have their own identity. But, according to the *sunyata* doctrine, they are, in fact, transient. Each is "like a bubble, a mirage, a dream, a magical show". All people and things in this "dream" are devoid of an abiding self or identity. What is in the world is really also not.

Buddhism recognizes that for most of the time we live in worldly reality, so we must stay in touch with the show of phenomena and lead compassionate, responsible lives. Once we comprehend that this reality exists only on one level, we can, through meditation, approach a perception of *sunyata*. As Sariputra meditated he became part of that joyful and boundless condition.

CHAPTER THREE

HEALING PRACTICES

There are many ways to practise Buddhism. You can affirm your faith daily by reciting vows. Chants and mantras calm the mind, and from there it is a simple step to meditation. Exercises and ancient texts can teach you how to develop your compassion for other beings. The rituals of Zen can bring clarity. Each of these paths is benignly healing.

Taking Refuge

It is traditional for Buddhists to affirm their commitment daily by chanting that they "take refuge" in the Buddha, the Dharma and the Sangha.

It helps to take refuge in the company of others. But you could speak the following words alone and still consider yourself part of the wider Sangha.

The words are given in Pali, the literary language of old Buddhism. It is just as good to speak them in English, but the sound of the Pali is beautiful.

Buddham saranam gacchami.	*I take refuge in the Buddha.*
Dutiyam-pi Buddham saranam gacchami.	*A second time I take refuge in the Buddha.*
Tatyam-pi Buddham saranam gacchami.	*A third time I take refuge in the Buddha.*
Dhammam saranam gacchami.	*I take refuge in the Dharma.*
Dutiyam-pi dhammam saranam gacchami.	*A second time I take refuge in the Dharma.*
Tatyam-pi dhammam saranam gacchami.	*A third time I take refuge in the Dharma.*
Sangham saranam gacchami.	*I take refuge in the Sangha.*
Dutiyam-pi saranam gacchami.	*A second time I take refuge in the Sangha.*
Tatyam-pi saranam gacchami.	*A third time I take refuge in the Sangha.*

Taking the Precepts

The five precepts are the guiding principles that form the framework of Buddhist ethical conduct. Lay Buddhists can recite these precepts when they visit a holy place, a monastery or a teacher, but they may also recite them daily to remind themselves of the fundamentals of Buddhism.

I vow to train myself not to hurt any being.

I vow to train myself not to take what is not given.

I vow to train myself to speak wholesomely and pleasantly.

I vow to train myself not to indulge in improper sexual pleasures.

I vow to train myself not to consume intoxicating substances which confuse the mind and cloud the judgment.

Living ethically

These precepts are easy to comprehend, but on close examination, they are also full of depth. Not every Buddhist is a pacifist. Some Tibetan monks and Zen samurai were fighting men. Nor is every Buddhist a vegetarian. Still, the injunction to non-violence and respect for all life stands central to Buddhism.

The second precept is a ban on stealing. Anything given freely may be taken. To take something dishonestly or against the wishes of its owner is contrary to Buddhist ethics.

The third precept suggests respect for other beings. And this rules out false, hypocritical or manipulative sweet talk, which is a variety of lying.

The vow to avoid sexual misconduct refers to how monks must renounce all sexual activity and lay people should conduct themselves with restraint.

In Buddhist terms mind-altering substances lead to the breakdown of awareness and self-possession. Only through awareness can one achieve insight into the *dharma* (truth). But so much cruelty and suffering result from intoxication, that this last precept also belongs in the realm of ethics.

Tibetan monks praying during the Saga Dawa festival, which celebrates the Buddha's enlightenment.

Monks and Laity

Buddhist monks and nuns give up owning, earning and producing food or goods. They have no homes and live with simplicity, and as celibate people. If this seems a bleak existence, it also has its wonderful freedom.

Abandoning the desire for wealth, fame and power, monks and nuns may focus on the experience of their own bare existence without worry or worldly clutter. There are, nonetheless, strict monastic orders that regulate a monk's day. They must eat their one daily meal before noon, and dress, sleep and speak to superiors according to strict monastic codes.

Mutual support

However, monks could not follow this lifestyle without the support of lay people. Every bowlful of food is donated. Robes, books, monastery lands and buildings must all be given. While lay people work to support them, monks and nuns reimburse what they are given in spiritual guidance, meditation training and moral teaching.

Perhaps most of all, the monastic community provides inspiration. Monks and nuns show how the Buddha's teaching remains alive and creative, while the lives of individual monks demonstrate the possibilities for spiritual development. These examples infuse lay society with a spiritual energy of its own. Lifestyles and responsibilities may differ, but together monks and laity form a community which is diverse, mutually supportive, and whole.

Vietnamese laity making an offering of incense in a Buddhist temple in Ho Chi Minh City.

Meditation

We all meditate in our own way. Palaeolithic people painted images in caves of the animals they worshipped. Tribal hunters wait for their prey for hours in silence and then strike with Zen-like immediacy. In Western society we may sit before a beautiful view and ponder our lives and the world around us.

The 19th-century author Herman Melville described another meditational state: "in the soul there lies one insular Tahiti, full of peace and joy, but encompassed by … the half-known life." Melville's "peace and joy" can be a product of meditation. Still more important is to illuminate, through meditation, the inner twilight of what Melville called the "half-known life".

Toward insight

The Buddhist Way can intensify the experience of meditation and deepen the results. Before his enlightenment, the Bodhisattva was watching a man ploughing. Observing the ploughman and his exhausted oxen and the worms and insects dying in their wake, the Bodhisattva was filled with compassion. Sitting down to meditate, he calmed his mind. "How dreadful," he concluded, "that ignorant people should not help fellow creatures who are also enmeshed in birth, suffering and death!"

The Bodhisattva's serenity and compassion brought him insight into the problem of suffering. And it is tranquillity and insight that remain the twin pillars of Buddhist meditation. The Buddha's words become our experience.

Starting Meditation

When you first start to meditate, you may experience a happy tranquillity as an end in itself. Once the process of meditation becomes familiar, you may move toward insight into the nature of suffering and existence. This exercise is a good introduction to meditation. Begin with 5 minutes. Practise each day and build up to 20 to 30 minutes.

1 Choose a time to meditate when you have eaten only lightly. Wear loose, comfortable clothing.

2 Retire to a place where you will not be disturbed. To calm the mind, first calm your entire being. Do a short exercise routine such as yoga, stretching or tai chi.

3 Adopt a comfortable but stable posture. Preferably sit cross-legged or kneel on some cushions.

4 Start with some long breaths in and out. Make the out-breaths thorough and relaxing. Gradually reduce the lengths of your breaths until you are breathing normally.

5 Focus your mind on the movement of each breath. When thoughts occur to you, note them mentally but return your attention to your breath. Alternatively focus your attention on the flower at the centre of this page.

6 Rest your mind at the point where each exhalation finishes.

Awareness

"Mindfulness" or "awareness" are the usual translations of the Pali notion of *sati* – a word thematically related to the term *buddha* ("awakened one"). As the Buddha himself outlined in a famous discourse, awareness meditation (later called *vipassana* meditation, see page 93) is the path to enlightenment.

The Buddha's teaching was direct and down-to-earth on this subject. In the *Satipatthana Sutta*, there is a beautiful description of how a monk should set about developing *sati*:

> "He must go to the forest, to the foot of a tree or to an empty place. He sits cross-legged with his body straight and arouses awareness of his breathing. Aware, he breathes in. Aware, he breathes out. Thinking, 'I breathe in long,' he understands that he breathes in long.... Experiencing the whole body, calming the activity of the body, he thinks: 'I shall breathe in'."

Extending our everyday awareness

The Buddha expressed the ordinary and non-mystical quality of this process vividly as he continued: "Just as a wood-turner who makes a long turn of the wood understands 'I turn long,' or when he turns short understands 'I turn short,' so it is with the contemplation of breath."

This comparison to the wood-turner brings home to us that meditation can be an entirely natural part of our daily lives. We can practise awareness meditation in a formal sitting posture, and also as we walk, lie down, eat and relate to the world and to other people.

Contemplation of the breath is a simple starting point of "contemplation of the body". As we become more experienced with meditation, we can start to look at other areas of the body and at our actions, mental processes and, in fact, the entire phenomenon of life and death. This, said the Buddha, helps us to live freely and to stop clinging to the things of the world.

The Buddha regarded the development of awareness as so important that he declared that it is "the one way for the conquest of suffering and the realization of *nirvana*". It may take a long time to achieve, but the practice is simple – everyone can do it.

A monk contemplates the raked gravel mounds of a Zen garden in Kyoto, Japan.

Contemplating your Surroundings

Even without formal meditation we can build contemplative moments into our days. These help to detach us from the nagging inner monologue of plans, memories and feelings.

One good contemplation exercise is simply to stand back and gaze at where we find ourselves. Suddenly the world jumps into brighter perspective and becomes more present, more solid. We see and hear things as they are. People and objects take on their own identities and become more than just the fuzzy backdrop to our own self-absorption.

We can practise contemplation almost anywhere, even in a stressful environment such as a traffic jam or a crowded waiting room. Wherever we are we will be learning to enter the world in a new way.

1 If possible find some pleasant, natural surroundings such as a garden or a park. Get into a comfortable position, either standing or sitting.

2 Look around you and choose an object to contemplate such as a tree, a plant or a building.

3 Gaze at the object's outline, proportions, colours and textures. Take in each detail in turn. Describe these to yourself in words. Note that the object has an independent existence.

4 Contemplate the object's place in time: its past, present and future.

5 Broaden your focus. Consider the object's physical environment.

6 Allow external reality to unfold its richness and power. Continue gazing for as long as you like.

Cultivating Non-attachment

Most of us live with attachments. We feel incomplete and cling to notions of future fulfilment, whether from wealth, fame, sex – even enlightenment. This attachment is an expression of the desires that underlie our discontent. When we are over-attached, we cling to fixed views, habit-forming rules and lazy rituals – Buddhist ones, too. But if we loosen our attachments, we grow in freedom.

The figure in the illustration is at once a part of and detached from the scene he contemplates. Detached also from conventional society, he is sufficient unto himself. He achieves liberation in time and space to simply exist within the great play of phenomena of which he is, serenely, a part. Use the following exercise to find a similar freedom.

1 Sit and contemplate something that is a major attachment for you. Do you want a promotion, a bigger house or a wider circle of friends?

2 Examine the thoughts and feelings that your attachment gives rise to. Does it make you feel envious, dissatisfied or incomplete?

3 Visualize a picture of yourself in relation to what you desire. Put some space between the two images. Gradually expand that space. As the space increases, relax in the freedom.

4 Practise this exercise regularly over the next few weeks. You may not lose your attachments. But you will learn to live with them with greater freedom, flexibility and self-knowledge. As the world changes, you can move with it.

Cutting through Delusion

Many Buddhists strive to achieve "right perception", a non-deluded view of the world and existence. But it is difficult to see the truth when our minds are restless and consumed by cravings and desires.

Much of what we do, such as working and caring for our families, is urgent and necessary. But we are also distracted by dreams of what we would prefer to be doing; these imaginary possibilities hide our view of the ultimate reality within us.

However, we all have the ability – if we make the effort to access it – to see beyond the flicker of events and restless preoccupations. Manjushri, the *bodhisattva* of wisdom, is both beautiful and sublimely fierce. Wisdom is represented by his sword, and it can help us to cut through ignorance and delusion.

1 Sit in your preferred meditation posture and breathe regularly. Gradually halt the flow of ideas and desires that is clouding your insight.

2 Visualize Manjushri as shown in the picture, right. See the beautiful serenity of his posture. Imagine the power of his upraised sword. It can sever the knots that bind us to delusion.

3 See the sacred scroll he holds in his right hand. Feel the radiance of its wisdom.

4 Imagine Manjushri's sword cutting through your delusions. Repeat the *mantra* of Manjushri: "*Dhi Dhi Dhi Dhi Dhi …*" Say: "May I obtain the wisdom of the Buddha. May my wisdom increase like Manjushri's."

Universal Love

The Buddha described "Four Sublime States of Mind" which would lead to rebirth in the highest of the Buddhist heavens. These states are equanimity (*upeka*), compassion (*karuna*), happiness in the well-being of others (*mudita*), and universal love (*metta*). Without insight, these do not lead to *nirvana*; but achieving these states brings great worldly merit.

Love for ourselves and others

That the Buddha shared what he had learned in itself represented an act of compassion. And anyone who follows the Way will reduce their own suffering and, by developing compassion, help to heal others – and, of course, learning to appreciate the experience of others also helps us to heal ourselves.

The Path of Purification, a meditation guide written in the 5th century CE, describes *metta* as "friendliness and the disappearance of ill-will" toward others. With great psychological insight, this guide suggests that we develop universal love by first directing it toward ourselves. Similarly an exercise in loving kindness, based on the Pali *Metta Sutta*, begins: "May I be happy and free from suffering!" After expressing the wish to be happy in yourself, you can go on to imagine the yearnings of other people for the same happiness.

In the second stage of *metta* meditation, we direct this universal love toward a loved one. The third and fourth stages, in which we radiate *metta* toward people for whom we feel indifference and hostility, are a harder challenge. But it helps to imagine that some of these people may have been our parents or children in previous lives.

> *"People who are skilled in good, who wish to achieve a state of calm should act thus: let them be easy to speak to, gentle, contented, serene, modest and not proud. … They should think: 'May all creatures be happy! Let no one work to undermine another. Let them never wish ill of another. Just as a mother would protect her only child, let people develop a loving heart for all beings!"*
>
> The *Metta Sutta*

Here is a beneficial and healing line to repeat silently or chant aloud in Pali:

> *Sabbe satta sukhito hontu!*
> *May all beings be happy!*

A large wooden statue of the compassionate goddess Kuan Yin dating from the Chinese Yuan Dynasty (1206–1368).

The Inner Tangle

Imagine a forest. The trees grow enormous, their foliage is dense and paths are obscured by creepers and bamboo thickets. Monkeys chatter and crash through trees. Carnivores and demons prowl the bushes. Images like these, of danger, chaos, discomfort and delusion, filled ancient Indian literature.

But the forest is also where the hero travels. At first lost in the jungle, at length he triumphs. Similarly Indian sages would sit and meditate in such half-lit seclusion; the darkness and tangle are where they sought illumination.

Finding a way out

But the forest is more than a setting. The self, before enlightenment, is a complicated tangle. The mind, say teachers, is a restless monkey, rushing from one impulse to another. The way out of this confusion is found in wholesome behaviour and meditation. These bring us to a place of peace, light and safety.

One of the gods came down to ask the Buddha: "There's an inner tangle and an outer tangle. This generation is entangled in a tangle. Who will untangle this tangle of tangles?" "Those established in morality and meditation," replied the Master, "untangle the tangle."

When we speculate about the future, when we worry, rush about and argue over this or that theory of existence, we also land ourselves in "tangles and thickets". When we quieten the mind and live simply and in the present, we find our direction. As we follow the Middle Way, the path becomes clearer.

Mantras

Mantras are mystic syllables that Hindus and Buddhists use to heal body and spirit, calm the mind and create exalted states of consciousness. The great Buddhist *mantra* is *"Om mani padme hum"*.

The simplicity and complexity of meaning

The syllable *"Om"* is, in fact, pronounced as a condensation of the letters "a", "u" and "m". These sounds can be recited in progression, one flowing into the other, and represent the complexity of waking, sleeping and pure dreamless consciousness. *"Mani padme"* are the two words that make grammatical sense. They mean: "jewel in the lotus". The silence that follows *"hum"* is a space of beautiful and intense consciousness. One translation of the *mantra* is: "Homage to the jewel in the lotus!" In other words, homage to the precious enlightened mind reposing within the purity of the Dharma.

Mani *(prayer) stones in Ladakh, northern India, inscribed with "Om mani padme hum".*

"Om mani padme hum" is the *mantra* of the Compassionate Bodhisattva, Avalokiteshvara. In Tibet and Nepal this is the *mantra* inscribed on prayer wheels (also called *Mani* wheels), which when spun activate the *mantra's* power and invoke the *bodhisattva's* love.

The entire Buddhist Dharma is said to reside in these mystic syllables, and his Holiness the Dalai Lama has explained that the three-part *"Om"* symbolizes our impure body, speech and mind as well as a *buddha's* sublime body, speech and mind.

Reciting the *"Om"* Mantra

Find a quiet place and get into a comfortable seated position. Start to recite *"Om mani padme hum"*. Intone each syllable slowly. Begin by repeating the *mantra* 20 times. Then, as you get used to it, build up the repetitions to 50 or more. A Tibetan rosary can help you to count. As you chant consider each part of the *mantra*'s purifying power, as summarized in this Tibetan teaching:

Om *will increase your generosity.*
Ma *strengthens morality.*
Ni *increases tolerance.*
Pad *energizes you.*
Me *boosts concentration.*
Hum *leads to wisdom.*

Chanting

A Tibetan manuscript of a ritual chant notation. The marks indicate patterns of rising and falling in the melody.

Nothing the Buddha said was written down in his lifetime, and he himself was non-literate, probably speaking Magadhi, a lost language. Soon after his death, the Buddha's followers met, and Ananda, his attendant, recited the Master's teachings (*sutras*) from memory, in the form of chants. Since that time *sutra* chanting has been a vital part of Buddhist devotion, and each Buddhist tradition has developed a special style. Theravadins (see page 12) of Southeast Asia usually chant in unison, accompanied on community occasions by pipes and drums. Japanese and Tibetan monks chant from deep in the abdomen, their voices often accompanied by bells and drums.

Finding Harmony

Anyone can chant virtually any Buddhist text. Short chants should be repeated three times, longer chants just once. The benefits of chanting are similar to those of controlled breathing (see page 92): chanting harmonizes the mind, body and breath and distracting thoughts drop away. Chanting also brings us in touch with the Buddhist Dharma. Although it is not necessary to use the original language, the ancient words carry a power and resonance that take us beyond literal meaning.

Try repeating one of the following chants three times. The first is an acknowledgment of your devotion to the Buddha. The second will remind you of the effects of your actions. Use Pali or English, whichever you prefer.

Namo tassa Bhagavato Arathato Samma-Sambuddhassa

Homage to the Blessed One, the Exalted One, to the Fully Enlightened One!

Kammassakomhi

Kammadayado

Kammayoni

Kammabandhu

Kalyanam va papakam va

Tassa dayado bhavissami

Evam amhehi abhinam paccavekkhitabbam

I am owner of my karma, heir to my karma,

Born of my karma, related to my karma.

Whatever karma I create, for good or ill,

Of that I will be heir.

Thus I should recollect.

Breath

Our breathing often expresses our physical and mental states. It comes short and fast when we are excited or angry and slows down when we relax. When meditating we can enter a condition of tranquillity by considering our breathing and the bodily movements associated with it. This awareness helps us to calm down physically and mentally. This, in turn, creates calmness in our daily lives and space in our minds for the growth of insight.

Meditating for Awareness

The following exercise relates to the first important stage in *vipassana* or "awareness" meditation (see page 76) and develops special attention to the breath. It will lead you to ever greater tranquillity and awareness.

1 Sit comfortably with your upper body straight. Bring your neck into alignment with your back. Practise long breaths. Notice how long breaths feel. Say: "I am breathing in long." Watch the long breaths.

2 Practise shorter breaths. Notice how these feel. Say: "I am breathing in short." Watch the short breaths.

3 Now breathe in a smooth, unhurried rhythm. Say to yourself: "I am breathing normally." Notice how it feels to breathe like this.

4 Continue to breathe in a normal and unhurried rhythm. Watch the progress of the breath from its entry at your nose through its descent through your chest and to your rising and falling abdomen.

5 Focus on the moment of stillness between breaths. Then observe the movement of your exhalation. Notice other thoughts that occur to you and let them go. Continue this exercise for around five minutes, or however long feels comfortable. Extend this time as you get used to this meditation.

Tao, the Way and Homeless Sages

The Chinese word Tao has been explained as "the Teaching" or "the Way", which nicely parallels the Buddhist "Path". Sometimes it is described as "Emptiness" or "the Absolute". But the *Tao Te Ch'ing*, said to have been written by Lao Tzu in the 4th century BCE, describes Tao in almost negative terms: "The Tao that can be told is not the constant Way." It is nameless, indefinable.

Experiencing Tao

Beyond description and inaccessible to conventional thought, Tao can still be experienced, and this is possible when we stop trying. Tao is everywhere, and the world's "ten thousand things" (all phenomena) emerge from it. To live simply in nature without ambition is to live freely in a timeless stream of Tao.

Because Tao is obscured by thought and action, it was said that "wise men should abandon learning and status". Seeking and producing nothing, they "merge with the world and move along with their surroundings". The Taoist master Chuang Tzu suggested:

> *"The man of intuitive wisdom lives quietly without exercising his mind. He performs actions without worry. ... He walks alone, but takes no pride in solitude. Rank and fortune are of no interest to him. The man of Tao remains unknown. The greatest man is No one."*

Living Tao

In pre-Buddhist China many lived this ideal. Some retired from work but continued living in busy communities, challenging custom and convention with sometimes outrageous – sometimes even drunken – subversiveness. Others, like early Ch'an (Zen) Buddhists, who were deeply influenced by Taoism, lived as wanderers and hermits.

The great T'ang dynasty poet, Han Shan, was an unknown and destitute recluse, whose descriptions of spiritual idleness on Cold Mountain – a metaphor for the Absolute – were both Taoist and Zen:

Cold cliffs, more beautiful the further you enter –

But nobody travels this path.

White clouds linger around the towering rocks;

On the green peak a solitary monkey cries.

What other companions do I need?

I grow old doing what I want.

Though face and shape change over the years,

I remain true to the pearl of the mind.

Han Shan, *c.*7th century CE

Early Zen Masters

Japanese Zen (Ch'an in Chinese) first appeared in southern China with the Indian monk Bodhidharma. He arrived in the 6th century CE, teaching a Mahayana doctrine (see page 12) which proclaimed that enlightenment lay within the mind, and that once we realize this we are all equally *buddhas*.

Spontaneous enlightenment

The transformative notion that we are born complete with a "womb" of spiritual realization within us is derived from the *Lankavatara Sutra*. But Zen teachers, starting with Bodhidharma, have almost invariably dismissed the study of texts as a hindrance. They believe that enlightenment can be achieved very suddenly, in meditation or through the tireless insistence of a teacher who pushes us to deeper insight.

In Zen thought enlightenment can also occur in the midst of performing commonplace activities such as sweeping a path or cooking. Hui Neng was perhaps the most celebrated master of the sudden-enlightenment school. Born in 7th-century China, he was a peasant boy when he joined a monastery as a wood-gatherer and servant. Pounding rice one day in the kitchen, the unschooled Hui Neng spontaneously grasped the essence of Ch'an emptiness, also called "no-self", doctrine. Hui Neng went on to become the Sixth Patriarch of Ch'an Buddhism, extending the practice and philosophy of the First Patriarch, Bodhidharma.

Cryptic sayings

Zen masters are famous for mysterious and poetic sayings designed to provoke spiritual revelation. The sage Teh Cheng was sitting idly in a boat one day as a high official passed. "What is this lazy priest doing?" asked the official. "Do you understand this?" responded the master raising his paddle. "I have been stirring the clear water, but a golden fish is rarely found."

Finding Buddha Mind

"The only reason I've come to China is to transmit the instantaneous teaching of the Mahayana: this mind is the Buddha. I don't talk about devotions or ascetic practices. Once you recognize your own nature, yours is the mind of all buddhas."

Bodhidharma, 6th century CE

Rinzai Zen Masters

"To pursue enlightenment is to obscure enlightenment," said the 9th-century Zen master Huang-Po, whose teachings led to the Rinzai school of Zen practice. "By seeking the Buddha nature, they [the unenlightened] lose it. For that is using Buddha to seek Buddha, using mind to grasp mind!" In other words it is useless to study, apply logic or even to make an effort. Buddhism is "ordinary, nothing special. Eat when hungry. Lie down when tired!"

In Rinzai Zen, as everyone has Buddha Mind, to realize this fact we must simply awaken. But the Japanese monk Hakuin (1685–1769) warned against laziness. "One often hears bald fools [monks] … say: 'Our minds are Buddha! There's nothing we need to do …' People like that are moronic heretics!"

18th-century Zen painting by the Japanese monk, Hakuin.

Irrationality and contradiction

To prevent students from thinking too hard, rather than using intuition, early teachers used seemingly irrational, and even violent, methods. Huang-Po answered questions from his student Lin-Chi with blows, not words. When Lin-Chi finally understood that this was, in fact, "grandmotherly kindness", he was awakened, and in acknowledgment he returned his master's blows.

Sometimes the masters spoke by contradiction. Mahayana doctrine teaches that all beings have Buddha nature. When asked if this included dogs, the Rinzai teacher Master Joshu shouted: "No!" To prevent his students from clinging to doctrines, he later answered the same question with a "Yes!"

Empty-handed and holding a hoe.

On foot, but riding a buffalo.

When the man has crossed the bridge,

It is the bridge that flows and the water
  that stands still.

Hakuin, 1685–1769

Like the empty sky: no boundaries.

But it is right here, profound and clear.

When you search for it, you will not find it.

You cannot grasp it:

But nor can you lose it.

It escapes you: but you catch it.

When you are silent, it speaks.

When you speak, it is silent.

The great gate is wide open.

And no crowd blocks the way.

Cheng-tao Ke, 665–713 CE

Zen *Koans*

Koans are problems or riddles based on the words of old Chinese and Japanese Rinzai masters, which are set for students as a means of meditation. By silencing mental chatter and propelling the mind beyond conventional ways of thinking, *koan* study leads into subtle realms of thought, which often seem to concern ridiculously mundane matters.

In one *koan* from a collection called *The Gateless Gate*, a monk asks the master Chao-chou for instruction. "Have you eaten your gruel?" replies the master. "Yes," says the monk. "Then wash your bowl!" retorts the teacher. Both encouragement and an insistence for more effort radiate from this conversation. Equally puzzling are other forms of *koans*, such as: "What is the sound of one hand clapping?" or "What was my face before I was born?"

STUDY A *KOAN*

Choose a *koan* from this page. Repeat it to yourself several times. Sit with the *koan* and allow its flavour to spread through your mind.

Continue with your daily activities, but keep contemplating the *koan*. Watch it gather special meaning. See how close you come to the incomprehensible.

Beyond confusion

Koan meditation aims first to arouse, and then to transcend, uncertainty. Hakuin quoted this ancient Chinese verse:

> *On the green mountain waves arise.*
>
> *At the bottom of the well, red dust dances up.*

"Study the verse, not the meaning!" warned Hakuin. "Then true great doubt will arise. If you struggle forward without losing ground, it will be as though an ice sheet has broken, a tower of jade has fallen!"

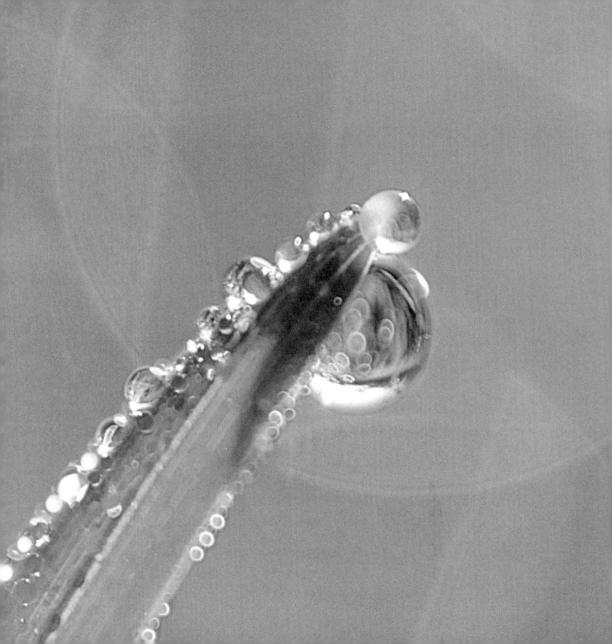

Dogen: Soto Zen Master

Soto Zen is known as the path of "just sitting". Repudiating ritual, a Soto Zen meditator "sits just to sit and walks simply to walk". The 13th-century master, Dogen, said that just to sit in meditation is *satori* (silent illumination).

Influential teaching

On returning to Japan after four years' study in China, Dogen retired to practise Zen in monasteries far removed from court and city life. His teachings have become philosophical and literary classics. Some describe exactly how to sit in meditation, and these texts can be fierce and demanding. Like the Buddha urging his students to "strive diligently", Dogen wrote:

> *"Zazen [Zen meditation] has nothing to do with intellect, volition or consciousness. ... Do not seek to become a Buddha! Do not waste your time! Be as fervent in* zazen *as you would be to extinguish a fire on your head!"*

By contrast many of his other writings are deeply poetic:

> *"Enlightenment is like the moon reflected on the water. The moon does not get wet, nor is the water broken. Although its light is wide and great, the moon is reflected even in a puddle an inch wide. The whole moon and the entire sky are reflected in dewdrops on the grass, or even in one drop of water."*

Buddhism and Social Action

A photograph published in 1963 of a Buddhist monk as he burned to death in protest against the political regime in his native Vietnam is one of the terrible images of modern times. This monk's cry was for higher political morality, and in that cause many Vietnamese students left home to join peasants in urgent development projects. Modern Cambodia, Burma (Myanmar), Sri Lanka and Tibet have been scarred by tragedy, too. But Buddhists from these countries have emerged with important messages of hope.

Voices of peace

One key figure is Thich Nhat Hanh of the Vietnamese peace movement. Nhat Hanh has had worldwide influence teaching the relevance of meditation as part of an engaged Buddhism: "Meditation is to see deeply into things, to see how we can transform the situation." By "situation" in this case he meant war, which results from "wrong perception".

In neighbouring Cambodia, working tirelessly for war victims, is the Venerable Mahaghosananda. As abbot of his Sangha, Mahaghosananda leads reconciliation in a society devastated by war and terror since the 1960s.

In the face of military repression, Aung San Suu Kyi, leader of the National League for Democracy in Burma and 1991 Nobel Laureate, has been another courageous human-rights advocate. Despite her many years under house arrest, Suu Kyi campaigns for "the protective coolness of peace and security" and for the "truth, righteousness and loving kindness" of Buddhist teaching.

The Dalai Lama

Perhaps the most famous advocate of world peace is the Fourteenth Dalai Lama. As a refugee from Tibet, he guides and inspires both his own Sangha in exile and a growing population of non-Tibetan followers.

Numerous Buddhists around the world have been moved by these teachers and others to engage in socially useful work. Prison teaching, human-rights and minorities' advocacy, environmental work and other compassionate activities, have become significant aspects of the modern Buddhist Path.

His Holiness the Dalai Lama is a tremendous living example of Buddhist compassion, and has been identified as an incarnation of the bodhisattva Avalokiteshvara.

CHAPTER FOUR

SACRED SYMBOLISM

Buddhism has a wonderful artistic tradition. While early Indian sculptors used symbols to depict the Buddha, later artists created masterpieces of imaginative portraiture. Zen painters and poets express visions of the world around them with the clarity and fervour of Buddhist insight. Similarly Buddhist temples and gardens radiate inner meaning.

The Face of the Buddha

Legend has it that two portraits of the Buddha were made during his lifetime, and that subsequent sculptures were copied from these. But the earliest representations of the Buddha were probably symbolic: a lotus representing his purity; and a footprint or a wheel suggesting the path of the Dharma.

Marks of greatness

A 7th–8th century face of the Buddha from Bihar, India.

Tradition tells us that the Bodhisattva was born with the 32 marks of the superhuman, and early images incorporated these, including: the long earlobes of Indian nobility; hair curling tightly in a propitious sunwise direction; a pointed head, manifesting wisdom; and delicate golden skin, suggested by polished stone.

Buddha sculptures of the Gupta period, in 5th-century India, also convey an idealized beauty. The face is aristocratic, serene and youthful; the half-closed eyes are lotus-shaped; while the full lips smile, as though bestowing confidence. Tibetan and Far-Eastern sculptures extended this devotional tradition, incorporating local ethnic features within the Indian prototypes.

Painting on plaster and other flat materials, the artist monks of Tibet and the Silk-Road kingdoms were inspired by classical Buddhist tradition and Hindu and local folklore. Tranquil Buddha faces are joined by sometimes ferocious manifestations of the Buddha Mind (see page 154), painted in gorgeous colours, with bulging eyes, surrounded by heavenly landscapes.

The Hands of the Buddha

Sacred hand gestures (*mudras*) long pre-date Buddhism. The hands and arms of Hindu deities express power, protectiveness and creativity, and many of their *mudras* may still be observed in postures used in yoga and dancing. In virtually all standing and seated depictions of the Buddha – when he is lying down, this refers to his death – the position of his hands is significant.

Expressing events and actions

The Buddha's gestures relate to events in his life or express symbolic actions. The "setting in motion of the wheel of Dharma" *mudra* in which the hands form a circle with the thumbs and index fingers touching, symbolizes the preaching of the first sermon. A seated Buddha with the fingers of his right hand extended to touch the ground shows the Buddha calling the earth to witness his enlightenment.

Expressing states of mind

Other important *mudras* express the Buddha's inner state and his relationship with others. When his right hand lies flat on top of his left, this signifies meditation. When the palm of his right hand faces forward and his fingers point upward, this expresses reassurance. When his right palm faces forward but the fingers point downward, this signifies giving – in some beautiful but rare variations of this, the Buddha holds a medicinal myrobalan fruit.

The *Bodhi* Tree

Three crucial events in the Buddha's life are associated with trees. According to legend his mother, Mahamaya, supported herself against a sal tree as she delivered the Great Being from her side. The Buddha later chose to lie down in a grove of sal trees as he approached death. But most famously it was at the foot of a great pipal tree that the Bodhisattva realized the Four Noble Truths, transcended the cycle of rebirth and entered living *nirvana*.

Symbol of the Dharma

Shrines to tree spirits and deities associated with trees have always been widespread in Indian culture, and the sages who taught the Hindu *Upanishads* transmitted their wisdom under the shelter of forest trees. But for Buddhists the pipal tree, with its broad, exquisitely shaped leaves has become known as the *bodhi* tree (literally "enlightenment tree") and is used as a supreme symbol of the Dharma.

Images of the Buddha seated at the foot of a *bodhi* tree occur throughout Buddhist art, representing his wisdom and compassion. And images of the tree by itself have come to symbolize the enlightenment event.

The site of the *bodhi* tree at Bodh Gaya, in the Indian province of Bihar, has attracted pilgrims since the 2nd century BCE. A stone seat marks the probable site of the tree, while a possible descendant of the original tree grows nearby, behind the magnificent 6th-century Mahabodhi temple.

The ancient Mahabodhi temple at Bodh Gaya was built on the orders of Mahanama, a Sri Lankan monk with royal connections.

The Lotus

With its glowing colours and luscious petals, the lotus filled classical Sanskrit poetry as a symbol of fertility and eroticism. However, this beautiful freshwater flower brings another meaning to Buddhist works: spiritual purity.

Among the Sanskrit names for the lotus, one of the most pungent is *punka-ja*, meaning "mud born". With its root in the foul but nutritious slime at the bottom of a pool, the stem of the lotus rises through the gloom and emerges to rest on the water's surface. There, in shining contrast to its muddy origin, the lotus opens in the sunlight, its petals unstained.

For this reason the lotus became a symbol of moral achievement and of the journey from ignorance to spiritual knowledge: the flower's untainted beauty and the devotee's appreciation of its progress through the darkness being of equal metaphorical importance. In the Mahayana tradition, the flower has extra significance: the complex "thousand-petalled lotus" represents the Buddha Mind (see page 154): the ultimate flower of realization.

The best, like lotus petals in a pool, are spotless.

Muddy water just runs off them.

They are never blemished.

The *Lalitavistara, c.*3rd century CE

Zen Painting and Calligraphy

Even as an expression of the Dharma, painting was regarded by some Zen masters as a distraction from the path of meditation. Nevertheless, the graphic work of the Chinese and Japanese Zen masters is perhaps the closest we can get to pictures of the enlightened condition.

Simply to write out sacred texts using carefully formed characters was regarded as a meritorious act. Many Zen monks explored the art further by making intentionally rough inscriptions on paper to express the "true essence of self" in spontaneous, sometimes deformed, "anti-calligraphic" strokes.

Some of the same energy radiates from portraits of Zen masters. Bodhidharma is drawn in several imaginary portraits with thick, crude lines, looking like a coarse lump of rock with grotesquely bulging eyes. Hui Neng, known as the Sixth Patriarch, is often drawn with rapid brush-strokes in the act of ripping up sacred texts – expressive of the "Crazy Wisdom" that was a frequent hallmark of Zen. Much of the Japanese painter Sengai's work, such as "Meditating Frog" and "Pointing at the Moon", is within this comic tradition.

Very different are the flower drawings and landscapes of later Zen painters. Plum blossom, orchids and bamboo were known as the "three pure ones" – symbols that express both the "suchness" and the impermanence of the created world. Perhaps the best-known Zen painter was the 13th-century Mu-Ch'i whose "Persimmons" and "Horse Chestnut" lead the eye into a still moment of meditation.

A hanging scroll painting of a mountain landscape, attributed to the monk Kei Shokei who lived in 16th-century Japan.

The Ox-herding Pictures

This series of ten pictures accompanied by explanatory paragraphs or verses originated in the Chinese Sung Dynasty (960–1279 CE). It illustrates a Zen parable outlining the stages on the path to self-realization.

The search

The story centres on a man who is searching for his stray ox – a symbol of ultimate reality. But the first frame challenges us at once with a Zen paradox: has the herder really lost his ox or did he have it all along? The herder then sights hoofprints – suggesting that the man has set out on the path of discovery, perhaps through study. The next two stages show both progress and a problem. The herder sights the ox – perhaps comprehending that he and the ox had never been separate – but he still needs to tame the creature.

Achieving enlightenment

The fifth stage shows the results of the herder's persistent efforts: the ox – the mind – is tethered and calm following behind the herder. By the sixth stage the struggle is over and the herder is riding the ox home singing. Herder and ox are moving effortlessly in the same direction, but they are still individual entities as the illusion of subject and object persists.

In the seventh picture, however, the ox disappears and the herder sits quietly in spontaneous illumination. This is followed in the eighth frame by an empty circle: the mind has dropped all its cravings and anxieties. In the ninth picture we return to a natural scene, as the herder's meditation deepens further and he impassively observes life grow and fall away. Finally, secure in his enlightenment, the herder re-enters society. Untainted by corruption, he frequents wine shops and fish stalls to bring buddhahood to everyone.

Poetry

Many traditions use poetry to express Buddhist themes. Sanskrit poetry, such as the 2nd-century *Buddhacarita* by Asvaghosa, excelled in beautiful narratives of the Buddha's career. The language is rich and exotic: Mara's assault, for example, is like "parasites of mind". By contrast Pali verse is plainer and more rooted in doctrine. The first verse, opposite, is a celebrated work by the 5th-century Indian writer Buddhaghosa that summarizes "no-soul" theory.

Ecstatic poetry

In a different genre are the ecstatic poems of Tibet's poet-saint Milarepa (1052–1135). Following a career in the black arts, Milarepa was initiated into the Dharma and for the rest of his 83 years he lived in remote caves where he composed exquisite descriptions of landscape and visionary illumination.

Zen poetry

Zen poetry, by contrast, is a contemplative art which evokes the "suchness" of transitory appearances. The greatest Zen poet was Basho (1644–94), who perfected the 17-syllable haiku in a colloquial language that expresses a world both changing and suspended in time. Basho's most famous lines, such as the first haiku opposite, seem to represent a *satori* experience (see page 103); while some later poems, such as the second haiku, express a melancholy vision. But Basho's successors, such as Buson (1715–83), saw joy in the world.

Suffering exists, not the sufferer.

Actions exist, but not the actor.

Nirvana is, but nobody is
    released.

There is a Way, but no one on it.

Buddhagosa

An old pond.

A frog jumps in.

Splash!

Basho

Resigned to death by exposure,

How the wind

Cuts through me!

Basho

In red rock jewel valley,

Fledgling sparrows learn to fly,

Monkeys leap and swing,

And animals run,

While I practise the path and
    meditate.

Milarepa

Young green leaves,

Water white,

Barley yellowing.

Buson

Tea Ceremony

The preparation of a bitter, green infusion, the offering to quietly appreciative guests, the meditative sipping ... these acts, along with a multitude of other, tiny formal gestures, comprise the unhurried Zen practice of *chanoyu*, the tea ceremony, which entered Japanese culture in the 13th century and to which the Zen monk Rikyu gave its ultimate form three centuries later.

The tea hut

"Form is emptiness and emptiness is form" proclaims the *Heart Sutra. Chanoyu* is both an art form and an expression of Zen emptiness. Ideally it takes place in a simple hut in a garden, to express both formality and elemental wildness. A pine tree, dripping water, bamboo thickets and carefully placed rocks surround the hut. Inside, to signify an unostentatious "poverty" (*wabi*), are straw mats, a hearth, an unpretentious vase holding a single flower, and an alcove where the host will hang a scroll showing Buddhist calligraphy.

Quiet appreciation

As the kettle hisses and the host pours water and whisks tea with ordered gestures, the guests admire the ceremonial utensils. Like the hut and its surroundings, cups, kettle and ladle are artfully "primitive". Finally, in harmony with this simple tranquillity, the host and guests sip tea in contemplative unity, while the wind whispers in the trees and water trickles over stones.

Tantra

Originating in 3rd-century Bengal, Tantra, also called Vajrayana ("Diamond–Thunderbolt Vehicle"), developed from a dramatic convergence of Mahayana Buddhism and non-Buddhist *yoga*. In contrast to the monastic Buddhism of the time, which often held out the prospect of enlightenment only after many rebirths in *samsara*, tantric Buddhism promised liberation in a lifetime.

Ritual practices

Tantra in its earliest forms was marked by vivid and unconventional rituals in which esoteric knowledge was transmitted to individuals and small groups by spiritual initiates (*siddhas*). In the course of these rites, *mantra* recitation, mystical diagrams and sometimes ritualized sexual intercourse were deployed to train the body, speech and mind to contact spiritual powers, and thus cut through delusion and psychological hindrances. The composition of these rituals was set out in deliberately abstruse texts called *tantras*.

Based on the thunderbolt sceptre of sublime buddhas, the vajra is usually paired with a bell to represent method or compassion.

Tantric symbols

A great symbol in Tantra is the *vajra*, the "diamond-thunderbolt" – "diamond" because of its durability and ability to cut through anything and "thunderbolt" because it illuminates the psyche in a flash. The *vajra* was an attribute of the sublime *buddhas*; but, in harmony with Mahayana thought, the power of the *vajra* was already inherent in the human mind.

Tantra draws on a repertoire of other imagery to express spiritual possibilities. In the "supra-mundane sphere" exist six heavenly *buddhas* and a galaxy of deities and demons, who represent aspects of the human psyche. Tantric adepts might visualize manipulating these beings as a way of altering their own spiritual make-up. When Tantra was carried to Tibet and Nepal in the 11th century CE, it fused with Himalayan shamanism to create new "skilful means" for the acquisition of wisdom and insight.

When you seek instruction in this practice,

Do not search for the scholar's knowledge.

If much knowledge is gained, this is the layman's way.

If this way prevails, a human life has gone to waste.

Master, student, instruction: these three.

Effort, courage, faith: these three.

Wisdom, compassion, absolute: these three.

Each of these is a constant knower of the Way.

Milarepa, 1052–1135 CE

The Union of Opposites

Oneness and duality, male and female, God and the soul: these are just three great opposites that Hinduism and Buddhism have explored in centuries of art and sacred writings. Repeating the *mantra* "I am that," the Hindu *yogi* works toward merging self with Brahman, the godhead. Even the Hindu gods, such as Shiva and Vishnu, conjoin with their female consorts to transcend their male eminence. So powerful is this notion of conjoined totality, that all-mighty Shiva is often portrayed as male and female in one.

Complementary counterparts

A Tibetan style yab yum image of two deities in a sexual embrace. The male represents compassion while the female represents wisdom.

The symbolism of these unified dualities was carried into Mahayana Buddhism. Avalokiteshvara, the male *bodhisattva* of compassion, is often depicted as female. And tantric Buddhism often portrays male and female deities locked in sexual intercourse. The male "wisdom deities" of the tantric pantheon all have cosmic *shaktis* (female powers), feminine counterparts who act in the world on behalf of suffering humanity.

The unification of wisdom and compassion is also symbolized in the hand gestures of the tantric goddess Prajnaparamita, a *shakti* of the Cosmic Buddha. Her finger and thumb are shown meeting in a beautiful circle, which expresses the interdependence of *samsara* and *nirvana*. This corresponds to the Mahayana insight that *samsara* and *nirvana* are, in truth, not opposites, but one and the same thing.

Visualization

Although it was awareness or *vipassana* meditation (see page 76) that eventually led the Buddha to enlightenment, he had previously studied and mastered concentrative yoga (*samadhi*), and this "one-pointed concentration" remained part of the Buddha's practice and became the concluding factor of the Eightfold Path.

To achieve an unshakeable state of *samadhi*, Indian Buddhists developed exercises in concentrative memorization. In one practice meditators would go to a secluded place and make a small disk of coloured earth, called an earth *kasina*. They would focus on the disk, then reproduce the image exactly in their mind and sustain it in their memory. Once such impressions can be controlled, practitioners are able to eliminate distraction and devote their whole attention to the exploration of Dharma.

Later Buddhists developed similar techniques to bring them closer to deities and *bodhisattvas*. Pure Land devotees (see page 152) visualize an image of Amitabha Buddha or a complex celestial landscape to reduce personal *karma* and to help them to achieve rebirth in the Western Paradise, Sukhavati. Practitioners of tantric Buddhism are initiated into a special relationship with a god protector (*yi-dam*) whose terror-inspiring aspect matches the initiate's impurities. Once the image of the deity has been repeatedly visualized, practitioners progress from their original impure condition toward integration with the deity's higher religious attributes.

Visualizing an Image of Love

Tantric visualizations should be practised only under a teacher's guidance. But you can still practise visualization to achieve a serene state of concentration.

1 Calm your body with 10 minutes of gentle exercise such as yoga, stretching or tai chi.

2 Sit comfortably in a quiet room. Place this image of the *bodhisattva* Maitreya in front of you.

3 Look at the image carefully for around 30 seconds, or as long as you feel comfortable. Absorb every detail.

4 Close your eyes and slowly build a mental image of Maitreya. Hold it in your mind for as long as you can. When the image fades, open your eyes and let them re-adjust.

5 Repeat the exercise. As you get used to it, prolong stage 4 for up to 20 minutes.

Temples

The Buddha believed in the gods, but he visited shrines perhaps more as a tourist than a devotee, and he might have wondered what later "Buddhist temples" were for. Nonetheless the growth of a temple tradition may be traced to the dwellings (*vihara*) that the Buddha himself used, which were donated by merchants and noblemen for each rainy season.

Within two centuries of the Buddha's death, meditation halls, *stupas* (see page 146) and shrines for the performance of devotion (*puja*) were added to these monsoon shelters. And similar sites became institutionalized in the 3rd century CE by the emperor Ashoka. From that point on monasteries became multi-functional centres where monks lived, taught and paid homage in shrines which sometimes developed into temples.

The great Indian Buddhist temples at Ajanta and Ellora, built in the 5th century CE, testify to later Buddhist communities, and the enormous Sri Lankan temple monastery at Anuradhapura was elaborated in the same period. With the spread of Buddhism, a vast variety of temples, both for meditation and *puja*, sprang up throughout Asia. Of the Chinese T'ang temples, the 8th-century Japanese temples of Nara and Kyoto, the immense Burmese complex at Pagan (11th century CE), Java's Borobudur (800 CE) and the exquisite Korean Silla Dynasty temples (8th century CE), many, but not all, have survived. Most recently the destruction of monasteries and temples in Tibet remains one of the religious and architectural tragedies of history.

The temple of Ta Keo, Angkor, Cambodia. The large tower in the middle represents the "temple mountain" at the centre of the universe.

Gardens

In the 10th century CE the Japanese nobility created gardens as places to retreat from court life. These were the basis for Buddhist temple gardens which became places for contemplation and objects of meditation in themselves.

Visions of paradise

The early temple gardens were influenced by Pure Land Buddhism (see page 152). Landscaped with its pond of clear water and fragrant, beautiful flowers around the central Silver Palace, Ginkakuji garden, near Kyoto, is a vision of the Western Paradise. Garden builders were also inspired by Chinese landscape paintings, with their rocks, trees and hermits' dwellings scattered through unpainted spaces. These depictions of the impermanent world and the emptiness of *nirvana* were developed into harmonious three-dimensional forms in gardens such as that of the Byodo-in temple, also near Kyoto.

Rocks rise from swirling gravel in a Zen garden in France.

Places of still meditation

Zen garden art reached its peak in late 15th-century Kyoto. Artificial and yet nakedly elemental, the most famous of these gardens is Ryoanji: an enclosed rectangle in which 15 carefully selected rocks rise like islands from a sea of raked sand and gravel. There are vantage points along the edges from which to contemplate the irregular and enigmatic calligraphy of the stones. *Samsara* and *nirvana*, emptiness and form, converge in these profound abstractions.

The Silk Road

The Silk Road is one of the world's oldest and longest trade routes, stretching from the eastern cities of the Mediterranean through Central Asia and India and finally to the old Chinese capital of Chang-an. All along this route metals, wool and precious stones from Europe were exchanged for Asian silk, jade and spices. But the caravans did far more than transfer material goods: the towns along the Silk Road became centres of cultural and religious exchange between Muslims, Christians and, not least, Buddhists.

In Buddhist terms the Silk Road has come to represent the spread of the religion from northern India and Gandhara (modern Pakistan and

A Pure Land image of the Western Paradise (see page 152) dating to c.618–907 CE, found in the Dun Huang caves, China.

Afghanistan) into China and eventually Korea and Japan. Indian monks first started travelling this route alongside traders around 300 BCE and are thought to have reached China in about 50 CE. According to one legend, the Han Emperor Mingdi dreamed of a golden figure floating in a halo of light, which his advisors told him was a vision of the Buddha. An envoy was sent to India to find out about Buddhism and he later returned with sacred texts and paintings and Buddhist teachers. More monks followed, and many Chinese people started to convert to the religion. Chinese Buddhists subsequently went on pilgrimage heading west along the Silk Road.

TRAVELLERS AND TEXTS

The most famous Silk Road pilgrim was the Chinese monk Hsuang Tsang, who travelled to India in the 7th century and returned with an influential collection of Buddhist texts. The story of his journey was hilariously fictionalized into the Chinese folk tale *Monkey*.

The archaeologist Aurel Stein followed his route in 1900 and made spectacular finds of artefacts preserved by the desert. Soon after, an even more extraordinary trove was found in caves outside Dun Huang, including the earliest printed book, a Chinese *Diamond Sutra*.

Pilgrimage

Shortly before his death, the Buddha suggested to his attendant Ananda that they visit the Capala shrine, which was near where they were staying. This sacred place was a shrine to local pre-Buddhist deities in a grove of trees, which the Buddha thought was "delightful".

The acquisition of merit

Buddhist pilgrims prostrating themselves at Bodh Gaya, India, where the Buddha was enlightened.

Around this time visits to shrines were a routine part of people's search for merit and fortunate rebirth. The Buddha appreciated the worth of this and instructed his followers to broaden the practice. Over the next two centuries, four sites associated with events in the Buddha's life became the focal points of Buddhist pilgrimage: his birthplace at Lumbini, his seat of enlightenment at Bodh Gaya, the deer park at Sarnath where he preached his first sermon, and Kusinara where he died. Visiting these sites remains a way of bringing the Dharma into tangible reality and deepening one's faith in the Buddhist path.

In the 3rd century CE the Indian emperor Ashoka, who made great efforts to propagate Buddhism, reinforced the pilgrimage tradition with a visit to Lumbini, where he erected a commemorative inscribed pillar. Shrines to other Buddhist elders extended the geography of pilgrimage. And once Buddhism spread east and north, travellers, such as the 11th-century Tibetan sage Marpa, took home Mahayana teachings from their pilgrimages. With their own acquisition of merit, they also spread the Dharma through example.

CHAPTER FIVE

SPIRITUAL COSMOS

Buddhist awareness is of the here
and now, but many Buddhists believe
that the time and space of individual
experience lies also within a universe
of deities and heavens of which our
world is just one part. These spheres
have enormous value as symbols
of the fruits of wholesome and
unwholesome action.

The Buddhist Cosmos

Early Buddhists were more interested in their spiritual condition than in myth or metaphysics. However, the Buddha did tell one spiritually beneficial creation story, which describes how the universe was once a sphere in which there lived beings who were "made of light" and "fed on joy", until greed caused them to lapse into a grosser form: humanity.

For a religion that centres on personal liberation, Buddhism has a complex cosmology. Over its 2,500 years of development in different societies, it has established a fascinating cosmological map of physical and spiritual worlds, including vast numbers of minutely differentiated heavens and hells. The following summary is common to most Buddhist schools of thought.

Map of the universe

At the centre of the Buddhist cosmos stands the mythic Mount Meru surrounded by four continents, one of which is Jambudvipa, "Rose-Apple Island", representing both India and the whole world of humans. Three other spheres comprise the remainder of the universe.

One of these spheres is the World of the Senses, which, in turn, contains six realms (see page 142) including heavens inhabited by gods, the demon world, the human world, an animal world, the world of "hungry ghosts" and a number of hells. Humans, depending on the extent of their *karma*, may be reborn into any of these worlds.

The two other spheres are referred to as the "higher" spheres and they are known as the Fine Material World of deities and an Immaterial World, where people who have experienced "unbounded space and consciousness" through concentrative meditation may be reborn.

One interpretation of *nirvana* even suggests that the Buddha's creation story can be reversed and that enlightenment can represent a return to the condition of those light- and joy-filled beings.

The Wheel of Life

Devotional paintings from the Tibetan Buddhist tradition often depict the World of the Senses (see page 140) as a Wheel of Life, a picture of the realms into which humans can be reborn. The six realms are in two main groups.

The fortunate rebirths

A Tibetan thangka (devotional painting) of the Wheel of Life, which depicts the human cycle of death and rebirth.

The upper half shows the three more positive areas. At the centre is heaven – a pleasant abode, but an area from which the gods rarely enter *nirvana* because their life of sensuality gives them no inclination to leave. To the right of this is the demon realm into which those possessed by anger are reborn. To the left is the human realm – a world of suffering, but the only world in which one can practise the Dharma.

The unfortunate rebirths

The lower half contains the three baser realms. On the left is the region of animals. People driven by ignorance, criminality and sexual immorality may be reborn here. In the centre are the hells, where burning or freezing are the fate of evildoers and those motivated by hatred. On the right are the ghosts, who are punished with hunger for lack of generosity.

Equally important are the figures in the innermost ring. Here greed, hatred and delusion are represented by a pig, a snake and a rooster endlessly chasing one another. The whole Wheel of Life is held by Yama, Lord of Death.

Mandalas

The Sanskrit word *mandala* literally means "circle". In both Hinduism and tantric Buddhism, *mandalas* are also sacred diagrams combining intricately patterned circles and squares. They are used as objects for meditation.

Key to the cosmos and the psyche

On a metaphysical level *mandalas* represent a many-layered universe, at the centre of which dwells a wrathful or sublime *buddha* or a depiction of Mount Meru, the hub of the Buddhist cosmos. The centre of the *mandala* is also a point of truth and resolution.

Around this lie the cardinal directions, each presided over by deities and *buddhas*. Intermediate areas of the pattern symbolize the elements of air, earth, fire and water as well as the possibilities and imperfections of the human psyche. The creator of a *mandala* or an adept who meditates on it thus enters into relationship with the Buddhist cosmos and gazes into a diagram of the human condition, with all its dynamic contradictions.

Physical and temporal aspects

The simplest *mandalas*, such as the Tibetan sacred mnemonics drawn on stones, are often impermanent. But, at their most complex, *mandalas* form the basis of temple architecture. Classic Hindu temple designs draw worshippers through a maze of courtyards until the worshipper stands face to face with the god in the innermost shrine. The Buddhist temple at Borobudur, Java, is built on a *mandala* pattern, with many levels and spiritual inhabitants rising to the central summit, which represents the Absolute and *nirvana*. In all *mandalas* the meditator is drawn in stages to this focal point, at which individuality and diversity are obliterated in an inexpressible condition of emptiness.

A Tibetan mandala dating from the 16th century.

Emptiness in all things

"When thought is realized as void and compassion, indistinguishable, that indeed is the Buddha's teaching of Dharma and the Sangha. As sweetness is the nature of sugar and heat of fire, so voidness is the nature of the elements. So it is said: through knowledge of samsara is nirvana."

Advayavajrasamgraha, 11th century CE

The *Stupa*

Stupas are monuments built to hold the relics of important Buddhist figures, and are places where monks and lay people can contemplate and worship.

These magnificent and elaborate buildings have a high-vaulted shape, which derives from mounds used for Hindu burials, and they all consist of three principal parts. At the base is a square platform, in the centre stands a dome, while a spire, often threaded by umbrella-shaped disks, rises at the apex. The base and dome are often faced with plaster and decorated with carved stone slabs. Apart from the reliquary chamber, the whole structure is solid and contains no habitable interior. The larger *stupas* are surrounded by paths, around which people can walk in the auspicious "sunwise" direction as they meditate on symbolic carvings and representations of the Buddha's life.

THE SYMBOLISM OF THE *STUPA*

The symbolism of the *stupa* is of fundamental importance. The earth that supports the edifice symbolizes the Buddhist virtue of generosity, the square base alludes to sensory restraint, the dome represents *nirvana* and the Buddha's final extinction (*parinirvana*), while the spire is a recollection of the Buddha's compassion. These can be contemplated in stages as people walk around the building.

The Buddha's relics

The Buddha had ordained that his remains should be preserved, and after his death the local rulers competed in an unseemly scramble to get a share. Eventually the relics were peacefully divided, but the *stupas* containing these have unfortunately been lost. Countless later monuments have been built to house the relics, bowls and robes of other Buddhist elders, and small-scale versions have been built for auspicious objects such as inscriptions.

Variations in design

The greatest Indian *stupas* were built at Sanchi and Amaravati (3rd century BCE–7th century CE). But there are fascinating variants in Burma, Thailand and Sri Lanka and in Tibetan *chortens*, which hold the remains of venerated *lamas* (senior monks). When *stupa* construction spread to the Far East, the umbrella disks on the spire developed into the segmented parts of the wooden pagoda.

Bodhisattvas

Bodhisattva is the Sanskrit (*bodhi-satta* in Pali) for "enlightenment being". In early Buddhist texts, the word refers both to Prince Siddhartha (see pages 20–23) before his enlightenment and to his previous incarnations. However, other *buddhas* existed before the Buddha, and still others will exist in the future. In the Mahayana tradition it came to be thought that there is also more than one *bodhisattva*.

On the path to enlightenment

In both Theravada and Mahayana thought there are several stages on the path to enlightenment. In the Theravada tradition, the final stage is that of *arahat*, the "worthy" or "perfected" one who will reach *nirvana* with the help of an enlightened teacher. Around the 1st century CE, innovators of the Mahayana tradition grew impatient with what they saw as inward-turning monasticism and an emphasis on individual salvation. Mahayana followers replaced the *arahat* ideal with the *bodhisattva*, a semi-mythological protective figure who transmitted the Buddha's wisdom and compassion to suffering humanity.

Bodhisattva qualities

There are two main differences between the *bodhisattva* and the *arahat*. First, while the *arahat* represents insight and renunciation, the *bodhisattva* qualities are wisdom, generosity and compassion. Second, the *arahat* moves toward *nirvana*, whereas the *bodhisattva* renounces *nirvana* until he has brought all other beings to the point of emancipation.

The most celebrated expression of *bodhisattva* generosity comes in the *Diamond Sutra*, in which a *bodhisattva* declares: "As many beings as there are in the universe … all these I must lead to *nirvana*." But *bodhisattvas* can achieve this only when they themselves have abandoned the notion of self, indicating that they are ready for *nirvana*.

A Tibetan statue of Avalokiteshvara. The bodhisattva *is often depicted with a number of arms and faces to show that he sees all, hears all and touches all.*

THE COMPASSIONATE *BODHISATTVA*

One of the best-loved *bodhisattvas* has always been Avalokiteshvara (Kuan Yin in Chinese; Kannon in Japanese), the Compassionate Bodhisattva. He – or sometimes she – has been represented in countless works of Buddhist art. The *Heart Sutra* describes Avalokiteshvara gazing down and analyzing the emptiness of phenomena in a harmonious mixture of love and insight.

Deities

The Buddha lived in a world filled with deities such as Vishnu and Brahma and minor spirits inhabiting local landscapes and shrines. But while the Buddha accepted the existence of deities – referring to the Heaven of Thirty-three Gods, for example – he regarded them as unenlightened beings who could not enter *nirvana* because they had not comprehended the Middle Way.

Unlike most religions, then, Buddhism started as a path in which gods were marginal. However, with the growth of Mahayana in the 1st century CE, a more populist Buddhism evolved. Based on devotion to a deified Buddha and a number of *bodhisattvas*, Mahayana Buddhism offered salvation to India's increasingly dispossessed urban poor. This new tendency became the basis for the deities of the Pure Land schools (see page 152), which evolved in 5th-century China and then in Japan.

Tantric deities

When the Buddhist missionary Padmasambhava arrived in Tibet in the 8th century, he agreed with the area's Bon religious leaders that local gods could be assimilated into the Dharma. The tantric pantheon thus became a wonderful amalgamation of Tibetan Bon and Indian Hindu deities. Even the wrathful deities depicted in Tibetan art are an essential component: some act as protectors of the Dharma, while others are personal guardians, with whose help devotees can transfigure imperfections into purity and insight.

Pure Land

Buddhists traditionally seek salvation from rebirth in *samsara* by following one of two paths: one is through "own power", or effort in meditation. The other, represented by Pure Land, is through the "other power" of faith.

The compassionate Buddha

This 18th-century Tibetan painting depicts paradises of purity and power, together with buddhas, bodhisattvas, lamas and primates.

Indian in origin, Pure Land Buddhism is a Mahayana sect that arrived in China in the 4th century CE. The movement's success lay in its promise of salvation through faith in the Compassionate Buddha of the Western Paradise. This *buddha* was Amitabha, or Amida, ("Infinite Radiance"), one of five celestial *buddhas* who dwelled in different quarters of the universe. The notion of the Western Paradise came from highly poetic Sanskrit texts, which described Sukhavati, a "place of happiness", where the faithful were reborn in ease and bliss, and where they could for ever hear the Buddha preach.

Reciting the sacred name

As Buddhism took root in China and then Japan, the promise of salvation had immense appeal to the poor who had neither the time nor the opportunity to study and meditate. To enter Sukhavati it was simply necessary to repeat the name of Amitabha with enough sincerity using the phrase "homage to the Amitabha Buddha" – a practice known as *nianfo* in Chinese or *nembutsu* in Japanese. Pure Land remains the most popular Buddhist sect in the Far-East.

A Pure Land hymn

Watching over the followers of the nembutsu,

In the worlds of the ten quarters, as numerous as dust particles,

He embraces and does not forsake:

Therefore he is called Amida.

Glossary

Amida a compassionate *buddha* who resides in the "Pure Land"

anatta Pali for "non-self"; teaching that rejects the notion of an intrinsic, unchanging entity at the core of a person

arahat an "enlightened being" of the Theravada tradition

Avalokiteshvara a *bodhisattva* whose name means "Lord who looks down in compassion"

bodhi Sanskrit for "enlightenment"

bodhi **tree** the pipal tree under which the Bodhisattva meditated until he achieved enlightenment

bodhisattva Sanskrit term for an "enlightenment being" who is destined to reach *nirvana*

Bodhisattva, the name that refers to Siddhartha Gautama before he became the Buddha

Brahma the senior member of the triad of supreme Hindu gods (Brahma, Vishnu and Shiva)

Brahman (or Brahmin) a member of the Hindu priestly caste

buddha an "awakened one" who has realized *nirvana* without the benefit of another *buddha's* teaching in his present lifetime

Buddha, the Siddhartha Gautama, the historical founder of Buddhism

Buddha Mind "ultimate reality"

Ch'an branch of Buddhism founded in China in the 6th century CE; reaffirmed the importance of meditation over scriptural knowledge and teaches that enlightenment can be found in one's intrinsic Buddha nature (see also Zen)

chanoyu Japanese tea ceremony

delusion spiritual ignorance and confusion; absence of awareness of the Dharma

dharma literally "duty"; also refers to Buddhist "teaching" or "truth"

Dharma, the the Buddha's understanding of eternal truth; the core of Buddhist thought

dukkha Pali term for "suffering" or "unsatisfactoriness"

Eightfold Path, the the Fourth Noble Truth and the way to enlightenment and *nirvana*

enlightenment full personal realization in mind, action and body of the Buddha's teaching

Four Noble Truths, the the Buddha's diagnosis of and cure for human suffering

Hinayana "Small Vehicle", refers to non-Mahayana traditions, including Theravada

karma Sanskrit for "action"; the law of cause and effect

karuna Sanskrit for "compassion", an ideal associated with *buddhas* and *bodhisattvas*

koan a riddle used by Zen teachers as a meditation aid

lama a spiritual teacher who has mastered tantric meditation

Magadhi ancient Indian language possibly spoken by the Buddha

Magadha Ganges valley kingdom in India of the 6th century BCE

Mahayana Sanskrit meaning the "Great Vehicle", a philosophical and/or devotional Buddhist tradition

mandala diagram of the cosmos and the self used in meditation

mantra mystic syllable(s); usually in Sanskrit or Tibetan

Mara Hindu God of Death, the Tempter or Evil One

metta Pali term for "universal love" or "loving-kindness"

Middle Way, the path between a life of extreme sensuousness or abstinence; the Fourth Noble Truth

Mount Meru mythological mountain at the centre of the Hindu and Buddhist cosmos

mudita joy at the happiness of others

mudra devotional hand gesture

nirvana Sanskrit for the "blowing out" of the flame of becoming; deathless state of peace; complete enlightenment

Pali a version of the Sanskrit language in which early Theravada texts were written

precepts moral codes or vows which Buddhists recite daily to affirm their belief

Pure Land a paradise where the good, but not the enlightened, may be reborn; Mahayana

Buddhist sect that believes salvation may be found here

puja Sanskrit for a devotional ceremony

Rinzai Zen sect which emphasized *koan* study and effort to attain sudden enlightenment; Japanese name of the school's 9th-century Chinese founder Lin-Chi

samadhi Sanskrit term for "concentrative meditation"

samsara "eternal wandering" through rebirth; ordinary, unsatisfactory reality

Sangha, the the Buddhist monastic community

Sanskrit ancient Indian language in which Hindu and Mahayana texts were written

satori the Zen experience of sudden enlightenment

shakti female consort of the tantric deities

Siddhartha Gautama the Buddha's personal name

Soto Zen sect founded by 13th-century master Dogen, which emphasized "just sitting" in

meditation to find one's intrinsic Buddha nature

stupa reliquary monument

sunyata Sanskrit for "emptiness"

sutra Sanskrit term for Buddhist discourse (*sutta* in Pali)

Tantra school of Mahayana Buddhism named after the *tantras*, texts considered to be the Buddha's secret teachings

Tao Chinese word meaning the Way or the Path

Theravada the "Doctrine of the Elders", a school of Buddhism formed in the first century after the Buddha's death

Vajrayana Sanskrit for "Diamond-Thunderbolt Vehicle"; branch of Buddhism also called Tantra

vipassana Pali term for "insight meditation" which aims to discipline the mind while fostering clarity about reality

Yama Hindu god of Death

yoga Brahmanic/Hindu religious discipline

zazen seated Zen meditation

Zen Japanese Mahayana tradition originating in Ch'an Buddhism

Further Reading

Basham, A.L. *The Wonder that was India*, Grove Press, New York, 1959, and Sidgwick & Jackson, London, 1985

Batchelor, S. *The Awakening of the West*, Aquarian, HarperCollins, London 1994

Bechert, H. and Gombrich, R. eds. *The World of Buddhism*, Thames & Hudson, London and New York, 1984

Carrithers, M. *The Buddha*, Oxford University Press, Oxford, 1983

Ch'en, K. *Buddhism in China*, Princeton University Press, 1973

Conze, E. ed. *Buddhist Texts through the Ages*, Harper & Row, New York, 1964

Conze, E. ed. *Buddhist Scriptures*, Penguin, London and New York, 1973

Coomaraswamy, A. *History of Indian and Indonesian Art*, Dover, New York, 1988

de Bary, T. ed. *Sources of Japanese Tradition*, Columbia University Press, New York, 1958

de Bary, T. ed. *Sources of Chinese Tradition*, Columbia University Press, New York, 1960

Dowman, K. *The Power-Places of Central Tibet*, Routledge, London, 1988

Dumoulin, H. ed. *Buddhism in the Modern World*, Collier Macmillan, London, 1976

Dumoulin, H. *Zen Buddhism – A History*, Collier Macmillan, New York and London, 1988

Eliade, M. ed. *The Encyclopedia of Religion*, Macmillan, New York, 1987

Fields, R. *How the Swans Came to the Lake*, Shambhala, Boston and London, 1986

Freemantle, F. and Trungpa, C. *Tibetan Book of the Dead*, Shambhala, Boulder, Colorado, 1978

Getty, A. *The Gods of Northern Buddhism*, Dover, New York, 1988

Goldstein, J. and Kornfield, J. *Seeking the Heart of Wisdom*, Shambhala, Boston and London, 1988

Gombrich, R. *Theravada Buddhism, A social history from ancient Benares to modern Colombo*, London, 1988

Harvey, P. *An Introduction to Buddhism*, Cambridge University Press, 1993

Johansson, R.E.A. *Pali Buddhist Texts Explained to the Beginner*, Curzon Press, London, 1977

Kitagawa, J.M. ed. *Buddhism and Asian History*, Macmillan, New York, 1989

Kitagawa, J.M. *Religion in Japanese History*, Columbia University Press, New York, 1966

Ling, T. *The Buddha*, Penguin, London and New York, 1973

Lowenstein, T. *The Vision of the Buddha*, Duncan Baird Publishers, London, 2000 and Thorsons, New York, 2003

Michell, G. *Penguin Guide to the Monuments of India*, London and New York, 1989

Murti, T.R.V. *The Central Philosophy of Buddhism*, Unwin, London, 1980

Nyanaponika, Thera *The Heart of Buddhist Meditation*, Weiser, New York, 1971

Nyanatiloka, Thera *Buddhist Dictionary*, Buddhist Text Society, Kandy, Sri Lanka, 1986

Rahula, W. *What the Buddha Taught*, Wisdom Books, London, 1990

Rawson, P. *The Art of Southeast Asia*, Thames & Hudson, London, 1993

Rowland, B. *The Art and Architecture of India*, Penguin, London, 1971

Snellgrove, D. *Indo-Tibetan Buddhism: Indian Buddhists and their Tibetan Successors*, Serindia, London, 1987

Snelling, J. *The Buddhist Handbook*, Rider, London, 1988

Stanley-Baker, J. *Japanese Art*, Thames & Hudson, London, 1991

Suzuki, D.T. *An Introduction to Zen Buddhism*, Rider, London, 1983

Suzuki S. *Zen Mind, Beginner's Mind*, Weatherhill, New York, 1972

Tharpar, R. *A History of India*, vol.1, Penguin, London and New York, 1974

Thomas, E.J. *The Life of the Buddha*, Routledge, London, 1975

Trainor, K. ed. *Buddhism: The Illustrated Guide*, Duncan Baird Publishers, London, 2001 and Oxford University Press, New York, 2004

Tucci, G. *The Religions of Tibet*, University of California Press, Berkeley, 1980

Tucci, G. *The Theory and Practice of the Mandala*, Rider, New York, 1974

Tworkov, H. *Zen in America, the Search for an American Buddhism*, Kodansha, 1994

Warder, A.K. *Indian Buddhism*, Motilal Banarsidass, Delhi, 1980

Warder, A.K. *Introduction to Pali*, Pali Text Society, Oxford, 1963

Warren, H.C. *Buddhism in Translations*, Atheneum, New York, 1979

Whitfield, R. and Farrer, A. *Caves of the Thousand Buddhas, Chinese Art from the Silk Route*, British Museum Publications, London, 1990

Wright, A.F. *Buddhism in Chinese History*, Stanford University Press, 1959

Yokoi, Y. *Zen Master Dogen*, Weatherhill, New York and Tokyo, 1976

Zwalf, W. ed. *Buddhism: Art and Faith*, British Museum Publications, London, 1985

Index

Picture Credits